KARATE-DŌ KYŌHAN

Gichin Funakoshi

KARATE-DŌ KYŌHAN

The Master Text

by

Gichin Funakoshi

translated by

Tsutomu Ohshima

KODANSHA INTERNATIONAL
Tokyo • New York • London

Distributed in the United States by Kodansha America, Inc., 114 Fifth Avenue, New York, N.Y. 10011, and in the United Kingdom and continental Europe by Kodansha Europe Ltd., Gillingham House, 38-44 Gillingham Street, London SW1V 1HU. Published by Kodansha International Ltd., 17-14 Otowa 1-chome, Bunkyo-ku, Tokyo 112, and Kodansha America, Inc.
Copyright © 1973 by Kodansha International Ltd. All rights reserved. Printed in Japan.
LCC 72-90228
ISBN 0-87011-190-6
ISBN 4-7700-0370-6 (in Japan)
First edition, 1973
92 93 25 24 23 22 21 20 19 18

CONTENTS

FOREWORD

I am highly honored that the family of Master Gichin Funakoshi, through Senior Shigeru Egami and Senior Genshin Hironishi, has permitted me to translate this book.

The translation has been ten years in progress, but unhappily the duration is no guarantee of the accuracy of my aim. Rather, it is a reflection of many interruptions and, above all, of my shortcomings in coping with English.

I release this translation at present with some misgivings and with a warning to the reader that I am still unable to read far without uncovering phrases that I feel could be rendered more clearly. I hope now at least that my most crooked turns have been made straight. My aim has been to remain as faithful as possible to the master's exact words. Such an attempt must at times put a strain on the English language since idiom frequently resists translation. A freer translation might have attempted, for example, to seek out English proverbs for Japanese expressions, but I think it would have forced a departure from the master's words and perhaps given rise to a distortion of his thoughts. I have sought to avoid this risk as much as possible; I have tried to keep myself and my interpretation outside of this work.

I should also mention that I cannot certify absolutely the accuracy of my rendering of some expressions which Master Funakoshi drew from Chinese literature. I regret that I was unable to locate all of these in their original form; perhaps someday I will be fortunate enough to have the sources identified.

Master Funakoshi worked on three different versions of this book: *Rentan Goshin Karate-jutsu* and two editions of *Karate-dō Kyōhan*. The second edition of the latter he did not live to complete himself. The three versions are close, but minor differences do exist. This work follows the first edition of *Karate-dō Kyōhan* in rendering the *kata*. Most of the master's students will see some variations from the *kata* as they have long been practicing them. Where possible, these variations have been pointed out in translator's notes. Such notes are to indicate that, customarily, given moves in the *kata* have long been done in the described manner.

I want to thank three persons who have struggled with me for long hours over this text: Harvard Itō, Don Ridgeway, and Caylor Adkins.

Master Funakoshi expressed the hope that his book would be improved on by later students. That thought may stand for this work as a translation.

TSUTOMU OHSHIMA

Tokyo
April 26, 1972

POSTHUMOUS NOTE
TO THE SECOND EDITION

The author, Master Gichin Funakoshi, seemed to be deeply troubled by the question of republication of this book. The feeling is clearly evident in his Preface to the Second Edition. Moreover, he was apparently concerned about whether he should republish the original text as such, or modify or extend it for the second edition. It has now been more than two years since the first announcement of the second edition appeared in the press, and we apologize for this long delay. The master passed away on this date one year ago without having completed the new manuscript. He must have regretted this fact deeply. Today, on the first anniversary of his death, we offer to his soul the completed manuscript, placing it on the altar and burning incense in his memory. We wish, in addition, to mention the forthcoming appearance of others of his manuscripts, including "Commentary on the Instructor's Manual," "Karate-dō for Boys and Girls," and "Essays on Karate-dō."

SHŌTŌKAI

Tokyo
April 26, 1958
On the first anniversary of the master's death.

PREFACE
TO THE SECOND EDITION

Twenty years have passed since publication of the first edition of *Karate-dō Kyōhan: The Master Text*. I recall with some feeling publication in 1922 of the earliest book, *Ryukyu Kempo: Karate*, and subsequent publication of the second, *Rentan Goshin Karate-jitsu*, which went to several editions. The honor afforded by the reading of the second book by the emperor and members of the imperial family was a source of deep gratification and humility to me. Then, after more than ten years of further training and experience, and about two years of review and correction of incomplete parts of *Karate-jitsu*, I published *Karate-dō Kyōhan: The Master Text*. The joy I felt at the appearance of this book remains as real to me as if its publication had occurred yesterday.

As a result of the social disorder that followed the end of World War II, the karate world was dispersed, as were many other things. Quite apart from a decline in the level of technique during these times, I cannot deny that there were moments at which I came to be painfully aware of the almost unrecognizable spiritual state to which the karate world had come from that that had prevailed at the time I had first introduced and begun the teaching of karate. Although one might claim that such changes are only the natural result of the expansion of Karate-dō, it is not evident that one should view such a result with rejoicing rather than with some misgiving.

It is, therefore, with mixed feelings of joy and remorse that I have watched and tried to provide a better direction to the course of the world of karate, and I am at a loss to estimate the influence I might yet exert upon its strongly flowing course. In any case, being now close to ninety years of age, it is not for me to speculate on the future. For several years, I have thought about the necessity of republishing this book. Recently, in attempting to locate a copy of the first edition in the large number of secondhand bookstores in the Kanda district of Tokyo, I was surprised at its scarcity and high price. Moreover, I have had many requests for a new edition from my students and am now convinced that there is still use for such a book among those who seek it. In approaching the writing of the new book, unlike my feelings before, I have been shocked by the profundity of Karate-dō to the point that even I at times have hesitated, and as a result the writing has extended itself over the past three years. Nevertheless, I have appreciated that if these profound aspects of karate are not set forth at some level now, they may never be built upon in the future, and it is with this recognition and with utmost humility that I provide this second edition.

To my students and to all others who devote their time to karate, may I express the hope that you will understand my earnest wish in this and will yourselves supplement this work; thus will the objective of the work be fulfilled.

GICHIN FUNAKOSHI

Tokyo
October 13, 1956

To search for the old is to understand the new.

The old, the new
This is a matter of time.

In all things man must have a clear mind.

The Way:
Who will pass it on straight and well?

Poem and calligraphy by Master Funakoshi.

CHAPTER 1
INTRODUCTION

Zōchō-ten, the guardian of the south of the Four Guardian Kings, symbolizes the *A* of *A-un*. His expression is that of the spirit of power released. Statue in dry clay. National Treasure. Tōdai-ji temple.

CHAPTER 1 INTRODUCTION

KARATE AND KARATE-DŌ

WHAT IS KARATE

In Okinawa, a miraculous and mysterious martial art has come down to us from the past. It is said that one who masters its techniques can defend himself readily without resort to weapons and can perform remarkable feats—the breaking of several thick boards with his fist or ceiling panels of a room with a kick. With his *shutō* ("sword hand") he can kill a bull with a single stroke; he can pierce the flank of a horse with his open hand; he can cross a room grasping the beams of the ceiling with his fingers, crush a green bamboo stalk with his bare hand, shear a hemp rope with a twist, or gouge soft rock with his hands.

Some consider these aspects of this miraculous and mysterious martial art to be the essence of Karate-dō. But such feats are a small part of karate, playing a role analagous to the straw-cutting test of kendo [Japanese fencing], and it is erroneous to think that there is no more to Karate-dō than this. In fact, true Karate-dō places weight upon spiritual rather than physical matters, as we shall discuss. True Karate-dō is this: that in daily life, one's mind and body be trained and developed in a spirit of humility; and that in critical times, one be devoted utterly to the cause of justice.

KARA 唐 AND KARA 空

Karate-dō is a martial art peculiar to Okinawa in its origins. Although it has in the past tended to be confused with Chinese boxing because of the use of 唐 in its earlier name, in fact for the past thousand years, the study and practice of masters and experts, through which it was nurtured and perfected and formed into the unified martial art that it is today, took place in Okinawa. It is, therefore, not a distortion to represent it as an Okinawan martial art.

One may ask why the character 唐[1] has been retained for so long. As I discuss in the section "The Development of Karate-dō," I believe that at the time the influence of Chinese culture was at its peak in Japan, many experts in the martial arts traveled to China to practice Chinese boxing. With their new knowledge, they altered the existing martial art, called Okinawa-te, weeding out its bad points and adding good points to it, thus working it into an elegant art. It may be speculated that they considered 唐 an appropriate new name. Since, even in contemporary Japan, there are many people who are impressed by anything that is foreign, it is not difficult to imagine the high regard for any-

1. The two characters 唐 and 空 are homonyms in Japanese. The first, 唐, denotes that that is foreign, in particular from ancient China, a meaning derived from its use in Chinese to signify the Tang dynasty (A.D. 618–907). The second symbol, 空, was introduced for the word karate and is now accepted as the correct one in this usage. [Translator's note.]

thing Chinese that prevailed during that period in Okinawa. Even at the time of the present writer's youth, lack of a full set of Chinese furniture and furnishings in one's home was a serious impediment to the social influence of any leading family. With this background, the reason for the choice of the character 唐, meaning "Chinese," as a simple case of exoticism is apparent.

Following tradition, the writer has in the past continued to use the character 唐. However, because of the frequent confusion with Chinese boxing, and the fact that the Okinawan martial art may now be considered a Japanese martial art, it is inappropriate, and in a sense degrading, to continue use of 唐 in the name. For this reason, in spite of many protests, we have abandoned the use of 唐 to replace it with 空.

THE MEANING OF KARA 空

The first connotation of 空 indicates that karate is a technique that permits one to defend himself with his bare hands and fists without weapons.[2]

Second, just as it is the clear mirror that reflects without distortion, or the quiet valley that echoes a sound, so must one who would study Karate-dō purge himself of selfish and evil thoughts, for only with a clear mind and conscience can he understand that which he receives. This is another meaning of the element *kara* in Karate-dō.

Next, he who would study Karate-dō must always strive to be inwardly humble and outwardly gentle. However, once he has decided to stand up for the cause of justice, then he must have the courage expressed in the saying, "Even if it must be ten million foes, I go!" Thus, he is like the green bamboo stalk: hollow (*kara*) inside, straight, and with knots, that is, unselfish, gentle, and moderate. This meaning is also contained in the element *kara* of Karate-dō.[3]

Finally, in a fundamental way, the form of the universe is emptiness (*kara*), and, thus, emptiness is form itself. There are many kinds of martial arts, judo, kendo, *sōjitsu* ("spear techniques"), *bōjitsu* ("stick techniques"), and others, but at a fundamental level all these arts rest on the same basis as Karate-dō. It is no exaggeration to say that the original sense of Karate-dō is at one with the basis of all martial arts. Form is emptiness, emptiness is form itself. The *kara* of Karate-dō has this meaning.

THE WAY FROM TECHNIQUES

The tremendous offensive and defensive power of Karate-dō is well known. Karate-dō is an art with which one can defeat enemies with a single fist attack or kick, without weapons. The value of the art depends on the one applying it.

---

2. The Japanese term for bare fists, 空拳 (*kūken*), combines 空 (*kara*) with the character for fist 拳. [Translator's note.]
3. In Japanese thinking, the hollowness indicates unselfishness; the straightness, obedience and gentleness; and the knots, strength of character and moderation. [Translator's note.]

If its application is for a good purpose, then the art is of great value; but if it is misused, then there is no more evil or harmful art than karate.

At one time, the police department of Okinawa attempted to introduce the art of karate to its members, but deep concern over the danger of this art caused the plan to be abandoned. In another instance, the late admirals Rokurō Yashiro and Norikazu Kanna proposed that navy personnel learn karate, but again fear that it would find application in sailors' brawls led to disapproval of the suggestion.

The indiscriminate use of the art of karate would cause great public concern and one cannot deny its potential dangers. However, it would be regrettable that pursuit of this mysterious art, of which one can be properly so proud, should be shunned simply because it is too dangerous. The source of concern is largely based on the misconception arising from instructors of poor character, who thoughtlessly place the emphasis of training on the techniques rather than on the spiritual aspects of the *dō*, and from the misbehavior and poor attitudes of karate students who are learning this art solely as a technique of fighting. There are even extreme cases in which students are actually encouraged to employ their karate in brawls. Such admonitions as "You can never improve or polish your techniques without some actual application in fights" or "If you cannot beat so-and-so, then perhaps you had better quit karate training altogether" are truly grievous for the reputation of Karate-dō. However, such talk only shows the lack of sense of those who know nothing at all about Karate-dō. Properly conceived and taught and practiced in the true spirit of Karate-dō, this art is not only the antithesis of a present danger but it in fact admits few equals as a thoroughly noble martial art (*budō*).

Powerful drugs are dangerous. Poison is frightening. However, there is no one in the medical world today who advocates shunning drugs. The danger of powerful drugs and poisons depends on their usage, and when applied correctly, they can be of great benefit. Karate-dō, improperly used, is certainly dangerous and vicious. But for the same reason that it is dangerous, karate, too, if properly applied, can yield results of great value. At the time a patient receives a prescription for a powerful drug, he is made to understand its nature and is taught its proper usage. In the same way, those who would learn Karate-dō must be made to understand it at the outset and be instructed in its proper use. The correct understanding of karate and its proper use is Karate-dō.

One who truly trains in this *dō* and actually understands Karate-dō is never easily drawn into a fight. One attack or a single kick determines life or death. Karate is properly applied only in those rare situations in which one really must either down another or be downed by him. This situation is experienced possibly once in a lifetime by an ordinary person, and therefore there may be an occasion to use karate techniques only once or not at all.

The writer has always told his students, "Art does not make the man, the man makes art." Students of any art, clearly including Karate-dō, must never forget the cultivation of the mind and the body. In Karate-dō, one's individual goal might be improvement of his health or training of his body to function efficiently. He might wish to develop the strength of his arms or legs or body, or to attain poise and spiritual fortitude. Clearly, one could wish to learn Karate-dō to become humble. All such goals have to do with self-development. In contrast, in the moment that one misuses the techniques, for example in fighting in such a way that he injures another or himself, or brings dishonor upon himself, he nullifies any of these benefits and merits of Karate-dō. Such misuse, arising from superficial understanding, is in fact self-defeating.

Through the man, techniques become art. I must earnestly repeat: do not misuse the techniques of karate.

True karate, that is, Karate-dō, strives internally to train the mind to develop a clear conscience enabling one to face the world truthfully, while externally developing strength until one may overcome even ferocious wild animals. Mind and technique are to become one in true karate.

Those who follow Karate-dō must consider courtesy of prime importance. Without courtesy, the essence of Karate-dō is lost. Courtesy must be practiced, not only during the karate training period but at all times in one's daily life. The karate student must humble himself to receive training. It may be said that a presumptuous or conceited person is not qualified to follow Karate-dō. The student must always be aware of and receptive to criticism from others; he must be constantly introspective and must readily admit any lack of knowledge, rather than pretending to know what he does not know.

Those who follow Karate-dō must never forsake a humble mind and gentle manner. It is the small-minded individual who likes to brag upon acquiring some small skill, and those with little knowledge who carry on as if they were experts are childish. It is because of the large number of false martial artists in the world that the public tends either to ignore the martial artist or to consider him wild. Therefore, many serious martial artists are embarrassed. Students of Karate-dō should always keep these points in mind.

Those who follow Karate-dō will develop courage and fortitude. These qualities do not have to do with strong actions or with the development of strong techniques as such. Emphasis is placed on development of the mind rather than on techniques. In a time of grave public crisis, one must have the courage, if required for the sake of justice, to face a million and one opponents. For the Karate-dō student, the most shameful trait is indecisiveness.

For many years, I have humbly dedicated my life to the introduction of Karate-dō to others. During the course of these many years, I have become associated with succeeding generations of fellow karate enthusiasts. Fortunately, my views have been understood by them, and their deep humility and gentleness have earned them the enthusiastic support of the public. I believe that this good result is a treasure we have found together through our mutual endeavor in karate.

In a few words, then, those who seek karate should not stop merely with the perfection of their techniques. Rather, I hope, they will dedicate their lives to seeking the true Karate-dō. This is because life through Karate-dō is life itself, public and private.

THE DEVELOPMENT OF KARATE

About fourteen hundred years ago Daruma (Bodhidharma), the founder of Zen Buddhism, left western India, penetrating mountain ranges including the Himalayas, and crossing unbridged rivers through complete wilderness, to travel to China to present lectures on Buddhism. Since even present roads between India and China would not be described as good, one can imagine the greatness of Daruma's spirit and physical strength—so great that he should have been able to conquer with such courage this difficult, several-thousand-mile way alone. In later years, as he traveled to the Shao-lin Temple (Shōrin-ji) in Hunan Province in China to lecture there on Buddhism, a great multitude of followers fell one by one in exhaustion from the harshness of his training. Daruma then set forth a method of developing the mind and body, telling them, "Although the way of Buddha is preached for the soul, the body and soul are inseparable. As I look at you now, I think it likely that you will not complete your training because of your exhaustion. For this reason, I shall give you a method by which you can develop your physical strength enough to enable yourselves to attain the essence of the way of Buddha." The method he set forth is contained in the *Ekkin Kyō* (*Ekkin "Sutra"*). With it, the monks were able to recover their spiritual and physical strength, and it is said that these monks of the Shao-lin Temple came to be known throughout China for their courage and fortitude.

In later times, after teaching of this method originally proposed by Daruma spread to many other places, it came to bear the name of its origin and was called Shōrin-ji Kempo. It was this method that eventually reached the Ryukyu Islands and developed into Okinawa-te, the forerunner of present-day karate.

Although there is no documentary evidence to clarify such points as dates of appearance or what original organizations existed, it is believed that karate must have come to Okinawa very early. Still, this *kempo* has come to be known as a martial art unique to Okinawa. About five hundred years ago, after the famous hero-king, Shō Hashi, united the three territories of Okinawa, a national policy was adopted under which the possession of any and all weapons by the people was forbidden. About two hundred years later (in the Japanese calendar, the fourteenth year of Keichō, i.e., 1609), weapons in the islands had been confiscated by the government, at the time when the Ryukyus came under the suzerainty of the Satsuma clan of Japan. It is supposed that the development of karate on the islands, as a means of unarmed self-defense, received tremendous impetus as a result of this double prohibition of weapons and through this developed into the Okinawan martial art of karate as we know it today.

There is no doubt that the many experts who traveled between Okinawa and China contributed heavily to the bringing of karate to its present level.

For example, it has come down by word of mouth that about two hundred years ago, a certain Sakugawa of Akata, in Shuri, traveled to China and then returned to Okinawa after mastering karate to become known as "Karate Sakugawa" during his time. Again, according to Shiodaira of Shuri, one hundred and fifty years ago (as noted in *The Ōshima Note*, by Tobe of Tosa, Japan), a Chinese expert, by name of Kū Shanku, arrived in Okinawa with a few of his students and introduced a type of kempo. Okinawan experts such as Sakiyama, Gushi, and Tomoyori, of Naha, studied for some time with the Chinese military attaché, Ason; Matsumura, of Shuri, and Maesato and Kogusuku, of Kume, with the military attaché, Iwah; and Shimabuku, of Uemonden, and Higa, Senaha, Gushi, Nagahama, Aragaki, Hijaunna, and Kuwae, all of Kunenboya, with the military attaché, Waishinzan. It is said that a teacher of Gusukuma, Kanagusuku, Matsumura, Oyatomari, Yamada, Nakazato, Yamazato, and Toguchi, all of Tomari, was a southern Chinese who drifted ashore at Okinawa.

In this manner, karate attained its fineness and became organized as it is today.

In more recent times, Master Tomigusuku received his training from Sakiyama, and Masters Azato and Itosu were students of Matsumura and Gusukuma, respectively. Masters Azato and Itosu were the teachers who instructed the writer, and to whom the writer is greatly indebted.

KATA

There is no end to distinguishing the various schools and styles of karate. As in the kendo and judo of years past, these various schools and styles are known by the names of the owners of the respective *dōjō*. In all budō, and not just karate, interpretations of the art by those who are training differ according to the interpretations of their instructors. Moreover it goes without saying that variations in expression are characteristic of each individual.

Nevertheless, if the kata are to be classified, then they fall broadly into either the Shōrei-ryū or the Shōrin-ryū. The former emphasizes primarily development of physical strength and muscular power and is impressive in its forcefulness. In contrast, the Shōrin-ryū (Shōrin "school") is very light and quick, with rapid motions to the front and back, which may be likened to the swift flight of the falcon. The Tekki Kata, as well as Jutte, Hangetsu, Jion, among others, belong to the Shōrei-ryū; whereas the Heian Kata and Bassai, Kwankū, Empi, Gankaku, and others are associated with the Shōrin-ryū. It is indeed impressive to watch a large-framed and heavily built man perform the Shōrei-ryū kata, overwhelming the observer with a display of sheer vibrant power. However, it tends to be somewhat lacking in quickness. Again, one cannot help but be greatly impressed in seeing a slightly built man with motions as quick as those of a bird in flight perform the Shōrin-ryū kata with techniques of a blinding swiftness, which are the elegant result of intensive training. Both styles, though, surely develop the mind and body, and one is not better than the other.

Both have their weaknesses and strengths, and those who would study karate should become aware of these points and study them accordingly. In addition to these kata, I have, as a result of several years of research into the general problem, developed two sets of kata, the Taikyoku no Kata, for beginners, and the Ten no Kata, to be used as matching (kumite) forms. I recommend that these kata be assiduously studied as well.

If all the various kata are considered, their number is very large. However, since the purpose of learning kata is not just for the sake of learning them but for the tempering and disciplining of oneself, it is not necessary to study indiscriminately large numbers of them. It should be sufficient for one to become familiar with the following nineteen kata and to continue to train in them exclusively. From the Shōrin-ryū kata, the beginner should study first Taikyoku Shodan, Taikyoku Nidan, and Taikyoku Sandan and follow these with Heian Shodan, Heian Nidan, Heian Sandan, Heian Yodan, Heian Godan, Bassai, Kwankū, Empi, and Gankaku. This is a total of twelve. From the Shōrei-ryū kata, one should study Tekki Shodan, Tekki Nidan, Tekki Sandan, Jutte, Hangetsu, and Jion. Including with these the Ten no Kata as kumite forms, one should obtain, I believe, the best use and expression of the various good points of the many kata. The many other forms will, therefore, not be treated here.

PUBLIC INTRODUCTION OF KARATE

Training in karate was always conducted with the utmost secrecy in Okinawa, with no one teaching or training openly in its arts as is done today. For this reason, books or written records on karate are almost nonexistent. It was naturally unthinkable that karate should be displayed in public exhibition. With the beginning of the Meiji period [1868-1912], the formal education system and the military conscription system were inaugurated, and during the physical examination of draftees and students, those young men with karate training were recognizable at a glance and greatly impressed the examining doctors with their well-balanced limb development and clearly defined muscular development. Then, some time later, the commissioner of public schools, Shintarō Ogawa, strongly recommended in a report to the Ministry of Education that the physical education programs of the normal schools and the First Public High School of Okinawa Prefecture include karate as a part of their training. This recommendation was accepted and initiated by these schools in 1902. I recall this to be the first time that karate had ever been introduced to the general public.

Shortly after the end of the Russo-Japanese War, in 1906, the author persuaded a few friends to form a group to give public demonstrations, and together we toured Okinawa. This was probably the first time that karate demonstrations had been held in public. In particular, at the opening ceremony of the new prefectural building, to which many nationally prominent people were invited, the writer was requested to lead a group of five outstanding masters of karate in a demonstration of this unique martial art. On another occasion, I was invited by the medical association to demonstrate and explain karate as a means of physical education. I also recall a demonstration before the students of the intermediate school of the city of Naha, and later these students themselves performed karate at a citywide athletic tournament, to the warm applause of the towns-people. During the years 1914 and 1915, a group that included Mabuni, Motobu, Kyan, Gusukuma, Ōgusuku, Tokumura, Ishikawa, Yahiku, and myself, as well as many other friends, gave many demonstrations, using the cities of Naha and Shuri as centers and going out from there to the surrounding areas. It was due to the ceaseless efforts of this group in popularizing karate through lectures and demonstration tours that karate became well known to the public, at least in Okinawa.

In either 1916 or 1917, the writer, continuing the promotion of wider appreciation of karate, was invited as the representative of Okinawa Prefecture to the Butoku-den in Kyoto, at that time the official center of all the martial arts, to give a karate demonstration. To my knowledge, this was the first time that karate, once for so long taught in secret, was to be demonstrated outside of Okinawa.

On March 6, 1921, the emperor of Japan, who was at that time the crown prince, visited Okinawa on his way to a European tour. For the occasion, karate was selected to be demonstrated before the crown prince in the Great Hall of Shuri Castle, and I humbly received the great honor and responsibility of the appointment to conduct the demonstration of karate by a select group of high school and college students. It was later gratifying to hear that the crown prince, upon being asked his impression of Okinawa, expressed particular pleasure with the beautiful scenery, the Dragon Drain of the Magic Fountain in Shuri Castle, and the mysterious elegance of karate.

In the early spring of 1922, the Ministry of Education held its First National Athletic Exhibition in Tokyo, and I was asked by the Department of Education of Okinawa Prefecture to arrange an exhibition of karate to be given at that event. I accepted the assignment and put my best efforts into the production of three large scrolls containing the history of karate and illustrations of its kata and techniques. I traveled to Tokyo with the scrolls as representative to the exhibition. I had hoped to return to Okinawa at the close of the athletic exhibition, but was strongly urged by several groups, the Shō family (descendants of the last king of Okinawa, Shō Tai), the Kodokan, the military academy, the bar association, the Society for Research in High School Physical Education, and more than ten other associations and organizations, to remain in Tokyo and to give a more detailed discussion of karate. Although I did not feel worthy of this task, I did believe it to be in the interest of karate and, therefore, made many trips about the country giving talks and demonstrations in an effort to popularize this art.

During this time, master artist Hōan Kosugi commented to me one day, "If you do return to Okinawa, we shall have difficulty in training for lack of instruction; could you perhaps leave something with us in writing explaining this way [dō]?" I was deeply moved by this request, and, having myself many times considered noting down some points about karate, I began then to devote my evenings to the writing of a book, which finally did appear, in November of 1922, with the title *Ryukyu Kempo: Karate*. This little book was the first published work on the subject of karate. Through it, karate, once transmitted in secret, was opened to the world. However, in the following year, the plates of the book were destroyed in the Great Kanto Earthquake of 1923, and this led to publication of a revised edition under the title of *Rentan Goshin Karate-jitsu* [Strengthening of willpower and self-defense through techniques of karate]. This edition was read by the emperor himself, an honor, of course, not only for me, but for Karate-dō itself. In other instances, at the end of 1924, I gave a demonstration at the Jichi Hall (Hall of "Self-Government") at Ueno, Tokyo, having qualified in the Tokyo Invitational Prize Contest for Athletics. On March 20, 1928, upon invitation of the Imperial Household Agency, I gave a demonstration with fifteen students in the Sainei-kan hall on the palace grounds.

Over the years, engrossed in my enthusiasm in explaining, demonstrating, and traveling here and there, I have been too busy to return to Okinawa. While I responded to requests for private lessons at the Meiseijiku [a *dōjō*] and continued to introduce karate to universities and business corporations, the time has slipped away, up to the present day. The universities with which I have been associated include Keio, Waseda, Shōdai,[4] Takushoku, Chuo, Gakushu-in, Hosei, and others. Additional major groups other than universities include the Matsuzakaya department stores and the Tokyu Department Store and Railroad Company. Other universities seriously studying karate include Meiji, Nihon, and Tokyo; and one can enumerate ten *dōjō* in Tokyo alone [1930s] offering karate instruction. Today, almost everywhere in Japan, I can hear the voices of karate training. Now, finally, karate has been introduced to far places abroad. As I look back over the past forty years to those days in the beginning when I was first introducing karate with my friends, it is indeed difficult for me to grasp the present widespread acceptance of karate. It seems as if it were a different period.

THE VALUE OF KARATE

AS ATHLETIC TRAINING

The nature of karate is such that it requires the body to move in all directions, in contrast, for example, to the emphasis on the arms in rowing or the legs in jumping. There is absolutely no need for concern about one-sided development of the body in karate, and the fact of uniform development may be considered to be one of the benefits of karate.

In most cases, only a minute or two is required to complete a kata. Moreover,

---

4. Shōdai (Tokyo Shōka Daigaku) is now Hitotsubashi University. [Translator's note.]

as one continues to practice, the movements become quicker and the training as a whole more vigorous, so that one can get ample exercise from a relatively short period of time. This is an ideal form of exercise for the many people today who complain that they would like to exercise, but they just do not have the time. The little time required is, therefore, a second major advantage.

Almost no other form of exercise, be it judo, kendo, archery, swimming, or horsemanship, can be performed at any time or place as easily as karate. Most sports require a large area, equipment, or a partner, and in this regard as well, karate is the most adaptable. No specific area, equipment, or even partner are necessary, for it can be performed in a garden, living room, hallway, at any time or place that one feels the desire to practice. This is the third significant advantage of karate.

Usually, exercise suitable for men is not suitable for women, and that for women is probably not enough for men; that for people recovering from illness is not enough for healthy people, and similarly, sufficient exercise for healthy, young people is too strenuous for older people or young children. Karate, however, may even be practiced by the physically weak, by women, children, and by elderly people. In other words, since each individual may adjust the exercise to his own capacity, and with each unit of exercise being of but one to two minutes' duration, there is no danger of overexertion or physical exhaustion. Moreover, as the body is built up and the techniques become more skillful, the movements naturally become more powerful, so that the amount of exercise becomes sufficient even for the healthy young man in his prime. Thus, the amount of exercise increases naturally as the training progresses, a point that I would cite as the fourth athletic merit of karate.

The fact that karate may be practiced either alone or in groups is a feature unique to it. Finally, even considered purely from the standpoint of physical techniques of practical value, the individual hand or foot movements, each with its own meaning, and the many variations in the various kata sequences become challenges to learn. While enjoying and being engrossed in their study on this basis, one accrues their benefits almost without realizing it.

The value of karate as physical training may easily be demonstrated by scientific tests, and even after a year or less of practice, one can easily see for himself the tremendous improvement in his condition over its state before karate training.

My esteemed teachers, the late masters Shishu (in Japanese, Itosu) and Azato, were both very weak in their childhood, but after starting to train in karate as a means of improving their health, they developed so much that they seemed like different people compared to their old selves and lived to become famous, in our times, as old masters. Master Shishu lived to the venerable age of eighty-five, and Azato to that of eighty. Master Azato's own teacher, Master Matsumura, lived to be over ninety years of age. Other contemporary karate experts such as Masters Yamaguchi, Aragake, Chibana, Nakazato, Yahiku, Tokashiki, Sakihara, and Chinen, have all lived to be over eighty. These examples are indicative of the role of karate as a superior method of maintaining one's health.

AS SELF-DEFENSE

Almost all living creatures have some mechanism for defending themselves, for, where this development is incomplete, the weaker are destroyed and perish in the fierce struggle for survival. The fangs of the tiger and lion, the talons of the eagle and hawk, the poisonous sting of the bees and scorpions, and the thorns of the rose and Bengal quince: are these not all preparations for defense? But if the lower mammals, birds, insects, and plants each have such specialization, should not man, the lord of creation, be prepared as well? An appropriate basis for the reply to this question is provided by the statement: We should have no intention of harming other people, but we must try to keep out of harm's way. To protect oneself, one must find a method that will give the weak the power to defend themselves against stronger opponents. The power of karate has become well known in these times for its effectiveness in breaking boards or cracking stone without tools, and it is not an exaggeration to assert that a man well trained in this form of defense may consider the whole body to be a weapon of awesomely effective offensive power.

Finally, although karate does have throwing techniques, it relies principally on striking, kicking, and thrusting techniques. These movements are much quicker and can escape the untrained eye. Block-attack combinations are executed simultaneously, and weaker individuals, women or young boys, do have ample strength to control a more powerful opponent with them. In short, among the advantages of karate as a means of self-defense are these: no weapons are necessary; the old or sick, or women, are able to apply it; and one can protect himself effectively even with little natural strength. These points combine to make karate a form of self-defense without equal.

AS SPIRITUAL TRAINING

Karate is no different from the other martial arts in fostering the traits of courage, courtesy, integrity, humility, and self-control in those who have found its essence. However, most of the martial arts, since their practice is harsh from the outset, are not suited to individuals of weak constitution, poor build, or weak character, and such students, generally speaking, will lose spirit and drop out early in their training. Moreover, it is possible for a student, because of physical weakness, to train so conscientiously that he overexerts himself to the point of injuring himself or becoming ill, his body not being able to keep pace with his will, and early failures of this sort are encountered as well. For these reasons, many people, being physically weak, have had to give up hope of training in the martial arts, even though such training and its development of bravery and a solid, firm body could be of special importance to the constitutionally or spiritually weak individual. It is, therefore, important in this context as well that karate can be practiced by the young and old, men and women alike. That is, since there is no need for a special training place, equipment, or an opponent, a flexibility in training is provided such that the physically and spiritually weak individual can develop his body and mind so gradually and naturally that he himself may not even realize his own great progress.

This flexibility of training also makes possible great strides in spiritual training. For if training in any martial art is discontinued after half a year or a year, it can hardly be expected to lead to any degree of spiritual training. An insight into this art, a mastery of its techniques, a polishing of the virtues of courage, courtesy, integrity, humility, and self-control to make them the inner light to guide one's daily actions: these require at the least ten or twenty years, if possible a lifetime of devotion to the study of this art. In view of its adaptability to continued training, I consider karate to be the most suitable of the many martial arts in leading to fulfillment of the need for training of the spirit.

CHAPTER 2
FUNDAMENTAL ELEMENTS

Master Funakoshi practicing
with the *makiwara*.

CHAPTER 2 FUNDAMENTAL ELEMENTS

THE HAND

THE FIST

It is so important in karate to know how to make a proper fist that it is necessary, before anything else, to understand thoroughly how to do this. The clenching of the fist can be represented as a three-step process. In the first step, the middle joints of the fingers are folded, in the second, the hand is folded at the basal joints of the fingers, and in the third, the thumb is placed so that its inner edge tightly grips the first two fingers. Figure 6 shows the front surface of the fist; the parts of the index and middle fingers forming this surface should be parallel and flat. Contact in striking should be made simultaneously on the four points marked in figure 6 on the joints and knuckles of the index and middle fingers. This type of fist is called the regular fist (*seiken*). Although it may be found somewhat difficult initially to make a proper fist, the difficulty is removed with a little practice.

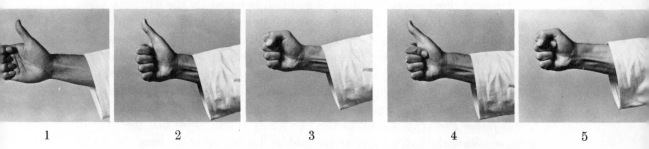

1 2 3 4 5

This is the fist most commonly employed in fist-thrust (*tsuki*) attacks. However, depending on the situation, one may also use the back of this fist (*uraken*) to attack the face of an opponent; or the combined heel of the hand and side of the little finger (*tettsui*), as shown in figure 8, against the face, elbow, or other parts of the body.

The condition of the fists is always maintained by regular practice with the *makiwara* (straw-covered post). The power and authority of the fists displayed in breaking boards and tiles are an incentive to conscientious practice with the makiwara. In practice, to strike the makiwara with the right fist, place yourself

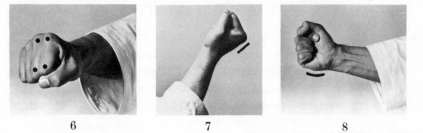

6 7 8

THE HAND 17

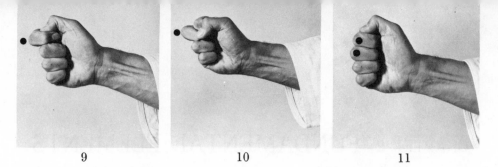

at a distance so that the fully extended fist just touches the makiwara. Draw the fist back and cock it above the hipbone with the fingers facing upward. The left foot should be placed forward, and the left arm extended to the front and downward with the fist six or seven inches above the knee in the left lower level block (*gedan barai*) posture described below. During the attack, the right fist rotates while advancing so that the back of the hand comes upward just at the instant of contact; the left fist is drawn back to the hip in the reversed rotating motion, which brings its fingers to face upward; and the lower abdomen is tensed with a sudden expulsion of breath, "uhmm!" (The training for this attack, the reverse punch (*gyaku-zuki*), is described on page 30.) Practice with the left fist as well, using the technique described and occasionally also an attack from the natural (*hachiji*) stance. Initially, do not strike too heavily or too many times, but practice lightly morning and evening. Gradually begin to use more force and increase the number of attacks, while becoming accustomed to the training and improving the technique through regular daily practice. Over a period of six months, increase the number of attacks to about one hundred times for the right hand and two hundred for the left (vice versa for a left-handed person). The trainee should be very careful not to give in to the youthful enthusiasm to strike the board either without plan or with too much strength. Overtraining not only can injure the knuckles, sometimes permanently, but it may occasionally be the cause of diseases of the internal organs. The point is to develop confidence in one's fists and to come to understand the relationship between the fist and hip.

One-finger Fist (*Ippon-ken*). In the two forms of one-finger fist, the joint of a finger, either the index finger or the middle finger, protrudes from the fist as shown in figures 9 and 10, respectively. Both forms require that the side of the thumb be held firmly against the index finger. This type of fist is employed primarily against the face, striking with the points indicated in the figures.

Flat Fist (*Hiraken*). As shown in figure 11, the four fingers are held together and bent so that they form a shallow fist, with the thumb being bent and pressed firmly against the index finger. This type of fist is used mainly against the face, the points used in striking the opponent being those indicated by the dots in the figure.

SPEAR HAND (NUKITE)

There are three ways of forming the fingers for the spear hand.

Four-finger Thrust (*Shihonzuki*). The most common is the shihonzuki, shown in figures 12 and 13; the four fingers are held tightly together and the thumb bent and held firmly in place. The back side of the open hand is not flat, the knuckles being bent and protruding slightly. The four-finger thrust is used

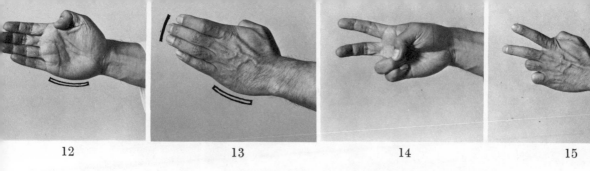

12   13   14   15

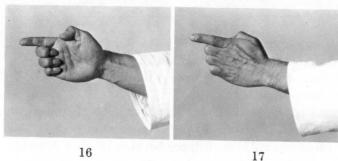

16   17

primarily in attacking the solar plexus of an opponent and can, with proper training, be more effective than the fist.

Two-finger Thrust (Nihonzuki). The ring and little fingers are closed, and the thumb is bent to lie on the top of the ring finger, as shown in figure 14. This is used only in attacking an opponent's eyes.

One-finger Thrust (Ipponzuki). As shown in figure 16, the one-finger thrust is very similar to the four-finger thrust except that only the index finger is extended. It is used in attacking an opponent's eyes. It might be mentioned that there is a method of training to toughen the fingertips for the spear hand, which consists of practice thrusts into containers of first rice and then, in gradual succession, beans, sand, and pebbles. However, there is no need for extensive training.

SWORD HAND (SHUTŌ)

The term shutō indicates the use of the hand as a sword. As in the spear hand, the four fingers are extended rigidly and the thumb is bent, but not too far, across the palm. The heel edge of the hand, as marked in figures 12 and 13, is used in striking the temple, between the eyes, the side of the neck in the region of the carotid arteries, or vital points on the arms, legs, and so on. Depending on the point of attack, this technique can also be more effective than the fist.

STANCES

There are seven stances (*tachikata*). They are the feet-together (*heisoku-dachi*), natural (*hachiji-dachi*), front (*zenkutsu-dachi*), back (*kōkutsu-dachi*), cat leg (*nekoashi-dachi*), horse riding (*kiba-dachi*), and T (*chōji-dachi*).[1]

1. The latest edition eliminates the T (*chōji-dachi*) and adds the immovable stance (*fudō-dachi*). This translation explains the immovable stance instead of the T. [Translator's note.]

18　　　　　　19　　　　　　20　　　　　　21

Feet-together Stance (*Heisoku-dachi*). As shown in figure 18, this stance is like that of attention except that the toes are together.

Natural Stance (*Hachiji-dachi*). This is the stance of at ease, with feet apart and toes turned outward.

Front Stance (*Zenkutsu-dachi*). As shown in figure 20, stand with one foot forward with bent knee. Have the feeling of pulling the front foot back and drawing the rear foot forward. The distance between the feet should be about three feet, with some adjustment for body height.

Back Stance (*Kōkutsu-dachi*). This stance is the opposite of the front stance (zenkutsu-dachi), the knee of the back leg is bent and the weight supported on the back leg. One should have the feeling of drawing the front foot into the back foot. The distance between the feet is about two and one-half feet with some adjustment for height. The lines of the two feet should intersect to form roughly an L.

Cat Leg Stance (*Nekoashi-dachi*). This stance derives its name from its resemblance to that of a cat about to spring upon its victim. The back leg is bent and supports the entire body weight, the toes of the front foot resting lightly on the ground. This stance enables rapid stepping either forward or backward and is also appropriate in kicking techniques.

Horse-riding Stance (*Kiba-dachi*). This stance resembles superficially the natural stance (hachiji-dachi). In assuming the stance, stand first with the toes turned inward, knees bent, and lower abdomen to the front. Now, lower the hips, hold the trunk erect, and, in applying stress, first to the thighs, as in horseback riding, then along the outer rims of the feet, tense the legs as if concentrating strength from their outer sides to the space between them; pull the heels inward until the feet are drawn almost parallel. Make a strong feeling in the lower abdomen. This is a very firm stance, and one who has mastered it does not fear (for example) even being swept away while standing on a rooftop holding a door aloft in a typhoon.

Immovable Stance (*Fudō-dachi*). This stance is formed from the zenkutsu-dachi by bending the back leg slightly and twisting the hips into a *hanmi* position (i.e., with the trunk rotated away from a full front position).

22　　　　　　23　　　　　　24　　　　　　25

HAND TECHNIQUES

HAND ATTACKS

Hand techniques (*tewaza*) consist of hand attacks (*tsuki-te*) and hand blocks (*uke-te*). Hand attacks include the regular fist (*seiken*), spear hand (*nukite*), sword hand (*shutō*), elbow (*empi*), single point (*ippon-ken*), back fist (*uraken*), and flat fist (*hiraken*). Hand and arm blocks include the scooping block (*sukui-uke*), hooking block (*kake-te*), pulling-in block (*hiki-te*), and sweeping block (*harai-te*).

Hand attacks (*tsuki-te*) is a general term used to describe various techniques.

Regular Fist (*Seiken*). In addition to its use in attacks, the seiken may also be used to divert or block an opponent's attack. The choice of parts of the body that serve as targets for it depends on the attack position of the opponent. Throughout the book, attacks will be broadly classified as being directed at the upper, middle, or lower level of the body.

Spear Hand (*Nukite*). The number of fingers used varies to provide one-, two-, and four-finger attacks. The spear hand is employed against an opponent's vital points. (See page 237.)

Sword Hand (*Shutō*). The hand and arm are employed in striking an opponent's attacking fist downward and in attacking vital points of the opponent's face, head, hands, arms, or legs. When one becomes proficient in this technique, it is at times more effective then the fist. (See page 19.)

Elbow (*Empi*). The elbow is used in striking an opponent's solar plexus, sides, chin, arms, and legs. When trained in this technique, even women and children may protect themselves quite effectively. Refer to figures 27–29.

Single-point Fist (*Ippon-ken*). The index or middle finger is bent to protrude beyond the rest of the fist to form a striking point. The single-point fist is used in attacking an opponent's temple, the point of the upper jaw just below the nose, between the eyes, and so on. (See page 18.)

Back Fist (*Uraken*). The back of the fist is employed primarily against the opponent's face. (See page 17, figure 7.)

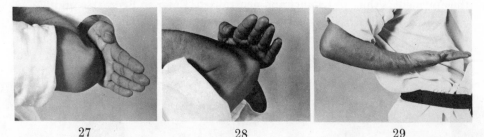

27   28   29

Hand and arm blocks (*uke-te*) include a variety of techniques employed in blocking or diverting attacking fists and feet. One distinguishes upper, middle, and lower level blocks, and additionally, for each level, an inside and an outside

30   31   32   33

type. In addition to those already mentioned, there are a vast number of individual techniques. The principal objective in all blocking is to maneuver the opponent into a disadvantageous position.

HAND BLOCKS

Scooping Block (Sukui-uke). This block is employed against both fist and foot attacks and consists of a scooping motion to block and throw, or block and catch, using the open hand or the fist. The technique throws the opponent off-balance and renders him ineffective after suppressing his fist and foot attacks.

Hooking Block (Kake-te). This technique is employed in blocking an opponent's fist attack. It occurs as the tenth step in the Tekki Shodan kata, in which the left arm executes a middle level (chūdan) hooking block (kake-te), the right arm simultaneously a lower level hooking block (gedan kake-te). It is possible to measure the degree of ability of an opponent by blocking his fist attack with a hooking block (kake-te) and then to adjust oneself accordingly.

Pulling-in Block (Hiki-te). This technique is a variation of the hooking block. In blocking the opponent's attacking fist, grasp the opponent's fist and attack while pulling him inward. His balance broken, the effectiveness of his attack is lost and that of the counterattack enhanced. A pulling motion coupled with a twist is much more effective here than a straight pulling motion (Figure 34).

Sweeping Block (Harai-te). This type of hand block clears the space between defender and attacker of attacking fists and feet. In contrast to the hooking block, the technique is executed with the feeling of knocking the attack out of the way. Refer to figure 35.

Trapping Block (Kakae-te). This technique involves grasping the opponent's attacking arm, pulling and locking it under one's own arm, and attacking while the opponent is thus off-balance and neutralized. Refer to figures 36 and 37.

Opening Block (Kakiwake). The fourteenth step of the Heian Yodan kata is the opening block. If seized, e.g., by the lapels, by both hands or attacked by both fists of an opponent, one breaks the hold or blocks the attack by a forceful

34   35   36   37

38   39

uncrossing of the wrists in the space between the attacker's arms, usually immediately following with a kicking or striking counterattack (Figures 38, 39).

Striking Block (*Uchi-te*). The striking block is used in both attack and defense. Attack vital points with the sword hand (shutō) or single-knuckle (ippon-ken) fist; or, alternatively, strike with the sword hand (shutō) or wrist to knock an attacking fist or foot out of the way. Once struck by a well-trained person who is able to crack an opponent's bones, an attacker loses much of his desire to fight.

FOOT TECHNIQUES

No other martial art has developed foot techniques (*ashiwaza*), to the high degree of refinement that they have found in karate. Indeed, foot techniques are a major strength of karate, and it, therefore, contains many different types. The following are those most often employed: front kick (*mae-geri*), side kick (*yoko-geri*) including both the side-up kick (*keage*) and side-thrust kick (*kekomi*) types, back kick (*ushiro-geri*), roundhouse kick (*mawashi-geri*), crescent moon kick (*mikazuki-geri*), stamp-in kick (*fumikomi*), knee strike (*hiza-tsuchi*), jump kick (*tobi-geri*), double kick (*nidan-geri*), returning wave (*nami-gaeshi*), and others.

Front Kick (*Mae-geri*). Beginners should start by taking the front stance (zenkutsu-dachi). Shifting the weight to the front foot, kick so that the rear foot follows the path indicated in figures 44 through 47. The striking point is the ball of the foot. Targets are the opponent's vital points and include the shins, groin, stomach, and chest. After sufficient training, the kick should be practiced from the natural stance.

Side Kick (*Yoko-geri*). As indicated, there are two types.[2] In the side-up kick

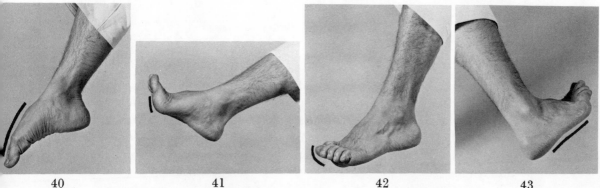

40   41   42   43

2. Originally the side-up kick was a low level kick. [Translator's note.]

44	45	46	47

(keage), the beginner should take the horse-riding stance (kiba-dachi). As shown in figures 48 and 49, kick upwards against the opponent's chin or attacking arm with the outside edge of the foot. In the side-thrust kick (kekomi), assume the horse-riding stance (kiba-dachi) and kick the stomach or chest of the opponent with the outside edge of the foot or heel, as indicated in figures 50 through 52.

48	49	50	51	52

Back Kick (*Ushiro-geri*). Upon being seized from behind by an opponent, kick immediately upward and toward the back with the heel. The targets of this kick are the testicles or shins. As the opponent backs away, lower the body and deliver an upward kick or thrust kick toward the back following the same principle as that of the side kick. See figures 53 and 54.

53	54	55	56

Roundhouse Kick (*Mawashi-geri*). Sidestepping an opponent's attack, twist the hips in a circular motion so that the toe or ball or instep of the foot swings inward at right angles to the opponent's body. The principle of the kick is similar to that of the front kick, but the difference in the body positions should be carefully noted. The correct position is that shown in figures 55 and 56 and 57 through 59.

24 FUNDAMENTAL ELEMENTS

57   58   59   60

Crescent Moon Kick (*Mikazuki-geri*). This kick is identical in almost all respects to the roundhouse kick. It differs in that the motion of the foot is a flatter arc, like the flat crescent of a new moon, from which the kick derives its name, and in that the striking surface of the foot is the sole. One who practices the roundhouse kick can execute the crescent moon kick without difficulty. The points of attack are the chest, stomach, and testicles. See figures 57–60.

Stamp-in (*Fumikomi*). Step in with great force, as if to cut through an opponent's body or leg with the outside edge (foot sword) of the foot. This motion is one type of the side-thrust kick (kekomi) and is used mainly against the opponent's knee, thigh, or instep to break his posture. See figures 61 and 62.

Knee Strike (*Hiza-tsuchi*). In grappling with an opponent, kick the testicles with the knee, or, pulling his head downward, kick the face with the knee.

61   62   63   64

Jump Kick (*Tobi-geri*). After evading an opponent's attack by leaping into the air to his side, attack his face or neck while in the air with a side-thrust kick.

Double Kick (*Nidan-geri*). This is another type of jumping kick. Leaping into the air with a bounding step, kick the opponent's stomach or testicles with one foot and then his face with the other (the jumping foot). Kicking with both feet while in the air is the characteristic of this technique. For a proficient person, this kick becomes quite high, and the expert can jump over an opponent's head

65   66   67   68

to take up a position behind him. Variations employ the side-thrust kick or roundhouse kick as the second kick in the air. See figures 67 and 68.

Returning Wave (Nami-gaeshi). This kick is the thirteenth step in the Tekki Shodan kata. The technique may be used, for example, to block an opponent's kick to the testicles if one's arms are locked. The sole of the foot is used to deflect the opponent's kick, and one continues by kicking the opponent's testicles or inner thigh in counterattack. See figures 69 and 70.

69   70

CHAPTER 3
BASIC TRAINING

Master Funakoshi executing *chūdan shutō-uke*.

CHAPTER 3 BASIC TRAINING

Before practicing the kata, learn well how to stand and how to kick. In order to move freely within the kata, one should practice, as part of the regular basic training (*kihon*), those techniques and stances that occur most frequently in the kata. One may say that the secret to rapid progress is contained in equal emphasis on the three categories of training: basic training (*kihon*), forms (*kata*), and engagement matches (*kumite*). The following are to be studied as part of training in basics: for the hand attacks, train attacking from a horse-riding stance (kiba-dachi) as well as practicing the reverse punch (gyaku-zuki) and front punch (oi-zuki); for the kicks, practice the front kick (mae-geri), side kick (yoko-geri), side-up kick (keage), side-thrust kick (kekomi), roundhouse kick (mawashi-geri), and double kick (nidan-geri); for hand blocks, include the down block (gedan barai), middle level sword hand block (chūdan shutō-uke), upper level rising block (jōdan age-uke), and so on.[1] There is, of course, no objection to practicing in addition other techniques found in the kata.

The kicks have already been treated in the section on foot techniques and will not be explained again, apart from stressing once more the importance of practicing both the left and right sides and not favoring one side over the other. For this purpose, if practicing in a place large enough, one should alternate series of left and right sides while practicing, working across the practice area.

Attacks from Horse-riding Stance (Kiba-dachi). As shown in figures 1 and 2, assume the horse-riding stance (if training in a group, at the command, "punching, ready"), cock one fist at the waist at a point above the hipbone with the

1   2   3   4

1. Master Funakoshi did not include the forearm block (*ude uke* or *uchiuke*) or the hammer block (*uchikomi* or *tettsui*) as part of basic technique, although these blocks occur many times in the kata. [Translator's note.]

fingers upward, and extend the other fist straight out to the front and center with the back of the fist turned upward and level with the wrist. Without changing the horse-riding stance, attack alternately with the right and left fists. Practice this repeatedly, so that the fists will attack straight to a target in the center at the front. It should be noted that the elbow of the attacking arm should not swing outside the width of the shoulder. To assure this, execute the fist attack from a cocked position at the waist with the arm sliding past the side of the body. In its cocked position, the fist always faces upward (i.e., with the fingers upward), rotating in a forward attack to bring the fingers to face downward at the instant of the strike.

Down Block or Lower Level Block (*Gedan Barai*). Although this is a blocking technique, it facilitates discussion to present the lower level, or down block, at this point in the order of study. Stand first in a front stance with the left foot forward and the left arm extended so that the fist is about six inches above the knee with the fingers upward. Similarly, when the right foot is forward, the right fist is forward. The trunk is set in a half-facing (hanmi) position to the right; that is, the hips are rotated about a vertical axis through about 35 degrees from the front. The trunk should not be leaning either to the front or the back, an important point that holds for all stances. Practice consists of repeated blocks while moving either forward or backward with each block. In either case, whether advancing a step with the right foot or retreating a step with the left, bring the cocked right fist diagonally up from the waist to the left shoulder and then swing it downward in a block synchronized with the leg movement. The left fist is drawn back to the waist at the same time to a cocked position above the hip, with the fingers upward. As indicated in figures 3 and 4, the down block is employed to block away a front attack from an opponent, and one should practice with this in mind. Practice both sides in this manner, alternating the one side with the other.

Reverse Punch (*Gyaku-zuki*). The ready (*yōi*) position for this technique is the down block posture. The attack is executed with the hips springing to a full frontal position from a half-facing (hanmi) position with the cocked right fist being thrust forward in a movement synchronized with the hips, as shown in figures 5 through 7. During the attack, the fist is rotated so that it extends to

5   6   7

30 BASIC TRAINING

the center in front with the fingers downward. Simultaneously, the left fist, which began six to seven inches above the left knee, is rotated and drawn back to be cocked at the waist with the fingers upward. The technique is called "reverse punch" because the forward foot and attacking fist are on opposite sides. In practicing an advancing series of right and left attacks, take a full step forward with the rear foot after completion of each reverse punch, drop the front fist to a point six to seven inches above the knee, and continue, as described, with the opposite fist. In a retreating series, take a full step backward with the forward foot after completion of each reverse punch.

Front Punch (Oi-zuki). The down block posture is the ready stance for this technique, as it is for the reverse punch. The essential points in this technique are similar to those in the reverse punch. The hips spring forward to a full frontal position from a half-facing posture, while the cocked fist is thrust forward and a forward step is made with the foot on the same side. Thus, as shown in figure 10, in an attack with the right fist, the right foot goes forward. This is a technique to be used in cornering an opponent and aggressively attacking him. Both the reverse punch and the front punch should be practiced with the feeling that the attack is executed primarily with the hips and lower abdomen rather than the arms and legs.

Middle Level Sword Hand Block (Chūdan shutō-uke). As shown in figure 11, one assumes the back (kōkutsu) stance at the command of ready (yōi). With the right foot forward, bring the right sword hand to a point above the left shoulder and swing it across toward the right side in a slightly downward motion of deflecting a front attack of an opponent. Stop the block with the elbow above the right leg, bent in a right angle and hooked slightly inward toward the body. At this point, the trunk should be erect, and the eyes, blocking hand, and forward foot directed toward the opponent. The hips should be in a half-facing position, and in one's practice, which consists of performing advancing or retreating series of alternating right and left blocks, the body should be set as if one were deftly parrying front attacks.

Upper Level Rising Block (Jōdan age-uke). The ready stance is similar to that for the down block. The arm extended over the front leg is raised in a concave motion inward and upward and then thrust upward with slanting forearm to block a blow to the face. After one block, one should block with the other arm in a similar manner, either advancing or retreating a step; the rising (blocking) arm and the withdrawing arm should cross each other in front of the face. This crossing motion is to be understood as the technique of grasping the attacking arm of an opponent with the blocking hand from the preceding block, drawing

BASIC TRAINING 31

| 13 | 14 | 15 |

it downward, and simultaneously attacking it from below by raising one's other arm forcibly into the crossed position.

In karate, there is no advantage to be obtained in becoming the aggressor. It is important that one's first move be that of warding off an attack, even though in practice this defensive act will have the character of an attack in itself. This is a principle realized through assiduous practice of blocking techniques.

CHAPTER 4
THE KATA

Taikyoku Shodan

Heian Shodan

Heian Nidan

Heian Sandan

Heian Yodan

Heian Godan

Bassai

Kwankū

Tekki Shodan

Tekki Nidan

Tekki Sandan

Hangetsu

Jutte

Empi

Gankaku

Jion

Ten no Kata Omote

Master Funakoshi and Senior Egami in demonstrations
of the kata. From the first and second editions.

CHAPTER 4 THE KATA

NAMES OF THE KATA

As I have already mentioned (page 9), instruction is usually given in the following nineteen kata (forms): Taikyoku Shodan, Nidan, and Sandan as forms for beginners; Heian Shodan, Nidan, Sandan, Yodan, and Godan, Bassai, Kwankū, Empi, and Gankaku, all of the Shōrin school; Jutte, Hangetsu, Jion, Tekki Shodan, Nidan, and Sandan, all of the Shōrei school; and Ten no Kata, as a kumite form.

The names of the kata have come down to us by word of mouth. Names in use in the past included Pinan, Seishan, Naifanchi, Wanshu, Chinto, and the like, many of which had ambiguous meanings and have led to frequent mistakes in instruction. Since karate is a Japanese martial art, there is no apparent reason for retaining these unfamiliar and in some cases unclear names of Chinese origin simply because of earlier usage. I have therefore changed those names I considered to be unsuitable after considering the figurative nature of the old masters' descriptions of the kata and my own study of them.

TAIKYOKU (FIRST CAUSE)

This is in fact three kata, numbered Shodan, Nidan, and Sandan. Since this form is the easiest of the kata to learn and consists of those blocks and attacks that are the most helpful in practicing basic techniques, it should be the form with which beginners start. This kata and the Ten no Kata to be described below are the product of my many years of research into the art of karate. If they are practiced regularly, they will result in an even development of the body and in a sound ability to bear the body correctly. Moreover, the student who has gained proficiency in basic techniques and understands the essence of the Taikyoku Kata will appreciate the real meaning of the maxim, "In karate, there is no advantage in the first attack." It is for these reasons that I have given them the name Taikyoku.

HEIAN (PEACEFUL MIND)

There are five Heian forms, containing a great variety of techniques and almost all of the basic stances. Having mastered these five forms, one can be confident that he is able to defend himself competently in most situations. The meaning of the name is to be taken in this context.

It is to be noted that the forms denoted here as Shodan (first) and Nidan (second) are reversed relative to their traditional ordering. The writer has introduced this change after consideration of their various points of difficulty and ease of teaching.

BASSAI (TO PENETRATE A FORTRESS)

This form contains repeated switching of the blocking arms, motions that represent the feeling of shifting from a disadvantageous position to an advantageous one, a feeling implying a will similar to that needed to break through an enemy's fortress.

KWANKŪ (TO LOOK AT THE SKY)

The name of this kata was derived originally from that of the Chinese military attache Kū Shanku, who introduced it. I have changed the name to the present one referring to the first movement of the kata, in which one raises his hands and looks up at the sky.

EMPI (FLYING SWALLOW)

The distinctive motion of this kata is an upper level attack following which one grasps the opponent and draws him inward, simultaneously jumping in and attacking again. The movement resembles the up and down and flipping away flight of a swallow.

GANKAKU (CRANE ON A ROCK)

Characteristic of this form is the one-legged stance occurring repeatedly in it, which resembles the splendid sight of a crane poised on a rock and about to strike down upon a victim.

JUTTE (TEN HANDS)

The remaining forms belong to the Shōrei school, and the movements are somewhat heavy when compared with those of the Shōrin school, but the stance is very bold. They provide good physical training, although they are difficult for beginners. The name Jutte implies that one who has mastered this kata is as effective as ten men.

HANGETSU (HALF-MOON)

In forward movements in this kata, one characteristically describes semicircles with the hands and feet, and the name is derived from this.

TEKKI (HORSE RIDING)

The name refers to the distinctive feature of these kata, their horse-riding (kiba-dachi) stance. In this, the legs are set in a strong, straddling position as if on horseback, and tension is applied on the outside edges of the soles of the feet with the feeling of gathering the strength in toward the center.

JION

This is the original name, and the character for it has appeared frequently in Chinese literature since ancient times. The Jion-ji is a famous old Buddhist temple, and there is a well-known Buddhist saint named Jion. The name sug-

B-3

gests that the kata was introduced by someone identified with the Jion Temple, just as the name of Shōrin-ji Kempo is derived from its connection with the Shōrin Temple.

TEN NO KATA (THE KATA OF THE UNIVERSE)

This form was introduced along with the Taikyoku Kata over ten years ago by the author. It consists of two complementary parts, front (*omote*) or part 1 and back (*ura*) or part 2, and the form is designed to be used equally well as a kumite form. Front (omote) is used in individual training and back (ura) in training with an opponent in matching (kumite). I hope that the student will study and practice it seriously until it has become a part of him.

ADVICE ON TRAINING

EFFECTS OF HASTE

In training, do not expect good results in a short time. Karate training may extend over one's entire life, beginning (although there is no actual age limit on starting) ideally in junior high school years. In the study of any subject, little is to be gained from haphazard training, and thus, particularly in a martial art such as karate, steady, unremitting training is required. Many people train furiously in karate initially but lose their enthusiasm even before the end of the first year. Clearly, very little good can be gained from such sporadic training, and, in fact, heavy training before the body is properly conditioned can result in injury to the body. One may even produce permanent injury to the body through this training whose express purpose is the development of the body. For these reasons, train systematically, without becoming impatient or overexerting yourself, and develop gradually, advancing steadily, one step at a time, with increased application of force and numbers of exercises practiced.

TIRING OF TRAINING

Many people become weary after training half a year or a year. This state of weariness, which is common and is not restricted to the study of karate, is a critical one, and a student may succeed or fail depending on his attitude during this period. Once aware of this state of languor, one must redouble his efforts and pass through this period with inspired spiritual effort. If he allows himself to become discouraged and quits at this point, his entire previous effort will be lost. The student who enters into this state of weariness shows that he actually does not understand and appreciate karate. Therefore, if he does quit training and gives up karate with only superficial understanding of it, it can properly be said of him that a little knowledge was a dangerous thing. Once you have begun karate for the benefit you might derive from it, it is my hope that you will continue to train thoroughly until you do come to a full understanding of it.

The most common causes of falling into this state of weariness are falling behind in training (compared with those who have started at the same time or later) as a result of sickness or injury, an inability to use the arms and legs as well as one wishes (as a result of insufficient time in training), or the lack of an appropriate partner to encourage one or to provide competition in training. Usually it is for these reasons that one finds a student becoming weary, losing interest and enthusiasm, balking self-consciously at practicing kata in front of others, lamely offering excuses such as, "I am not really suited for karate," and, finally, quitting altogether. Conversely, the best way to progress is to keep to a schedule of regular practice each day, to continue even after having fallen behind one's peers (because one catches up with them easily with time in any case), firmly to set high goals, and to practice steadily without rushing or becoming impatient. In order to maintain one's interest and enthusiasm in karate, he should try to attain a thorough insight into karate by appreciating kata performed by others, by listening to the points of view of others on karate, by reading books, and especially by attending exhibitions of karate as often as possible, as well as practicing with the *makiwara* and other training equipment. If the student returns again and again to ponder on karate, he is able to avoid this sort of weariness.

INDIVIDUAL TRAINING

It is a unique feature of karate that it can be practiced alone and at any time and in any place. Insofar as possible, one should wear light, informal clothing similar to that worn in normal daily activity. An area of about nine by twelve feet is appropriate, which can be reduced after some training to nine by six feet. Until one has learned the order of the kata, he should concentrate on this rather than on applying much strength. After understanding the basic structure of the kata, one should then gradually apply more strength. Finally, once he has completely learned the order and acquired a feeling for the kata, he should then begin study of the next kata.

GROUP TRAINING

Although individual training in karate can be of great interest, there is also pleasure in group training. As in other forms of exercise, there is a characteristic good atmosphere associated with training under the direction of a leader of a group at a school, club, or other self-development organization.

HOW TO STUDY THE KATA

In the past, it was expected that about three years were required to learn a single kata, and it was usual that even an expert of considerable skill would only know three or at the most five kata. Thus, in short, it was felt that a superficial understanding of many kata was of little use. The aim of training reflected the precept expressed by the words, "Although the doorway is small, go deeply inward."[1] I, too, studied for ten years to really learn the three Tekki forms. However, since each form has its particular good points and because there is also benefit to be gained from knowing a wide selection of forms, one might well reconsider the practice of becoming deeply engrossed in very few forms. Where-

1. This expression suggests that one develops his being, spiritually and physically, through longer and deeper study and practice. [Translator's note.]

as people in earlier times made deep studies of a narrow field, people today study widely and not deeply. It is not a good idea to follow one way or the other; it is better to take the middle way. For this reason, I have employed the method of advancing students as soon as they have a good grasp of a form to the next one, up through the fifth Heian form or the third Tekki form, and of then returning to the first for renewed practice. Once a form has been learned, it must be practiced repeatedly until it can be applied in an emergency, for knowledge of just the sequence of a form in karate is useless.

SPECIAL SKILLS AND WEAKNESSES

Just as everyone has a favorite form and also forms in which he is particularly weak, some individuals have an especially strong fist attack or sword hand technique, others rapid kicking technique, or particular skill in jumping techniques, for instance. It is desirable that each student practice his favorite techniques and polish them to the highest degree, but he must at the same time avoid concentrating on these techniques to the exclusion of those he likes less. In blocking an opponent's fist attack, for example, there are situations in which one should block with the hand and other instances where a foot block is appropriate; and similarly, among the hand blocks themselves, different situations require a deflecting block, a downward block, a scooping block, a drawing-in block, or a hitting-pushing-aside block. One must, therefore, know all the various blocks and understand their respective applications so that he is able to employ the correct block for each particular position, stance, and attacking technique presented by his opponent. Certainly, any student with the vapid notion that would lead him to feel, "My favorite block is the down block and there is no need for me to learn any other block," is a very shallow thinker indeed, for it should be obvious that just as a down block has its strong points, so does every other block. One must therefore learn to distinguish strong and weak points, to make comparisons among them and to study them. If the instructor is not competent, it is particularly easy for the student to fall into these bad habits in sparring practice. For this reason also, I recommend that one emphasize kata practice and train for sparring only secondarily.

TRAINING PERIOD

With respect to the length of individual training sessions, a period of about ten minutes is appropriate for most people. After acquiring skill and experience, one may at times train for an hour or longer, depending on his physical strength. He should be cautioned, however, that excessively long training sessions, prompted by youthful ardor, are to be avoided. Ideally, one who has time should divide his training into morning, noon, and evening sessions. The technique exists for the man. At the very least, karate training is an endeavor in continued self-improvement, so that it would be the height of folly to impair one's health or become ill through injudicious training. One should, therefore, keep in mind that it is better to train frequently, even for short periods, than to have long but infrequent sessions. In any case, recalling that a kata requires only one or two minutes to complete, he should think about practicing before breakfast, after lunch and supper, when he is fatigued, during a work break at his desk, at any time and any place.

THREE CARDINAL POINTS

Three points should be kept in mind during karate practice: (1) light and heavy application of strength, (2) expansion and contraction of the body, and (3) fast and slow movements in techniques. Although there are those who in their karate practice apply strength excessively or indiscriminately in rapid motions, application of great strength does not indicate rapid progress in learning, and the use of strength in continuous, rapid motions does not mean that one is skilled. Rather, in doing the kata one must learn to apply strength where it is called for and not otherwise, to move quickly when necessary, and to slow down when appropriate. The most important factors underlying proper regulation of strength and speed are the three points enumerated here. In a given kata, in order really to apply the points, degree of strength, expansion and contraction of the body, and fast and slow movements of a technique correctly, it is necessary that one fully understand the particular features of this kata and the meaning of each technique in it. Only after drinking in deeply the significance of these three main points will one be able to practice the kata correctly.

LEARNING NEW FORMS

Since it is difficult to learn an entire form in a single session, it is better for one teaching or learning a new form to divide it into several sessions. For instance, one might distribute it over three sessions, taking the first half during the first session, the second half during the next, and then the entire form as a unit during the third. Having learned the sequence of the form, one should then begin to correct the respective stances and posture, come to understand the meaning of each of the movements, and concentrate on application of the three points, the light and heavy application of strength, expansion and contraction of the body, and fast and slow parts of a technique, in the form. Progressing in this way should create interest and provide for a natural learning of the form.

ARRANGEMENT OF SUBJECT MATTER

In general, while learning any subject, one should start with its easier aspects and advance to more difficult ones; that is, begin with the simple and reach for the complex. This is, of course, applicable to karate, which should be learned in an orderly fashion. In the past, it was true that many of the experts taught their favorite forms first to their students. This was probably the result of their knowing only about three forms; thus, the practice could be traced partly to a lack of subject matter, and it may have misled their students. The present writer has stressed organization of subject matter in the design of this book with these points particularly in mind and has arranged the book in the light of his past fifty years of experience. For this reason, he does feel that this book can be a proper reference for beginners in karate.

LINE OF MOVEMENT

The pattern described on the floor during performance of a particular kata is called the line of movement (*embu sen*). The lines of movement of all of the kata may be grouped roughly into the five types illustrated below.

These five types are approximate, and deviations from them will be pointed out as they occur in descriptions of the individual forms. In preparing to do a particular kata, one should first of all note its line of movement and take his starting point accordingly. For example, in forms whose line of movement is the straight line, one might need room either to the sides, as in the Tekki forms, or in front and behind, as in Gankaku. In particular, performance of a kata in an exhibition may become awkward if this point is not kept in mind.

"Whatever goes must come back": in karate, the points at which one starts and completes the kata must coincide, and failure in this indicates either that an incorrect step has been taken or that variation in lengths of stride has caused deviation from the correct positions. Since karate depends in a very real way on the stability of the hips and not just on the use of the arms, length of stride and positions of the feet must be practiced with particular thoroughness. Whatever goes will return: it is in order to facilitate the assimilation of this rule that in each figure referring to the kata the position of the corresponding step is indicated relative to the line of movement, and one must adhere strictly to these diagrams in practice.

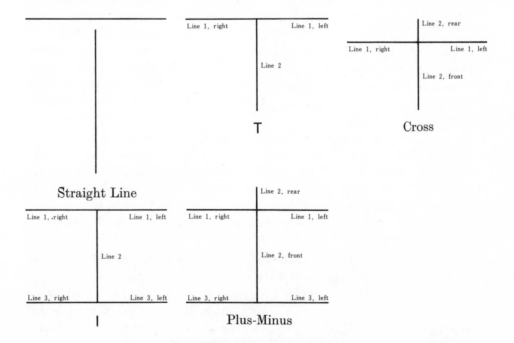

THE KATA

Before presenting the forms, I shall explain various symbols employed with the figures. The figures show sequentially the stances and movements in the kata, and are numbered consecutively for each kata. Supplementary pictures providing detail have the upper left corner removed. A circle in the upper left corner indicates a customary practice different from that described in the first edition. Coordinated with the figures are sketches of the appropriate positions of the feet relative to the line of movement. Numbers in boldface type below the footwork diagrams relate them to the numbered paragraphs describing the kata. In the diagram, a solid footprint on the line of movement indicates the position of the foot at the moment in the form illustrated by the figure, whereas an outlined footprint denotes the position of the foot in the preceding stance. In those cases where part of the foot is not touching the floor, that part is white. A dotted line indicates the path of the foot motion.

Although it is really very difficult to learn a kata well, I do believe that a student may have confidence that he will attain a substantial level in karate even through self-study if he practices diligently according to the explanations and figures given in this book.

TAIKYOKU SHODAN, NIDAN AND SANDAN

There are three Taikyoku forms (numbered by the ordinal terms, Shodan, Nidan, and Sandan). Taikyoku Shodan is an elementary form consisting of two arm techniques, lower level deflecting block (gedan barai) and middle level front attack (chūdan oi-zuke), and one stance, the front stance (zenkutsu-dachi). Because of its simplicity, the kata is easily learned by beginners. Nevertheless, as its name implies,[2] this form is of the most profound character and one to which, upon mastery of the art of karate, an expert will return to select it as the ultimate training kata.

Once one is able to perform the Taikyoku forms with proficiency, he can understand the other kata with relative ease. For this reason, the Taikyoku form should be considered elementary as well as the ultimate form. In fact, the Taikyoku Kata is the very prototype of a karate kata, a combination of the the down block and middle level front punch (basic techniques in any training), the front stance, the typical body movements of karate, and a defined line of movement.

The line of movement of Taikyoku Shodan is of the I category. The kata consists of twenty-four movements and the ready (yōi) and yame positions. Beginners take about forty seconds to complete the form, whereas an advanced student should shorten this to five or six seconds. It is worthwhile to note that

2. Taikyoku is a philosophical term denoting the macrocosm before its differentiation into heaven and earth: hence, chaos or the void. [Translator's note.]

1   2   3   1   4   2

the I category is the most basic of the lines of movement, the others being derived from it.

Yōi. It is proper to bow before and after performance of the kata. Following the bow, one positions the fists about two inches in front of the upper thighs, the fingers toward the thighs. The eyes are fixed directly to the front, the chin in, the shoulders lowered slightly in a natural posture; the lower abdomen is flexed slightly, the legs are straight without being locked at the knees, the right foot is about a half step from the left, and the toes are pointed outward slightly in a V (natural stance). The yōi[3] stance is an integral part of any kata, and one's level of ability is already clearly evident from this stance. One must, therefore, approach this stance with a very serious attitude.

1. Pivoting on the right foot, advance a half step along the left branch of Line 1 with the left foot, at the same time swinging the left fist downward, like a pendulum, in a circular motion starting above the right shoulder and centered on the left elbow, and blocking at a point five to six inches above the left knee. During the motion, the right fist is pulled back to a point above the right hip, as shown in figure 3. The left knee is bent and the right leg fully straightened. The trunk should have the standard posture of the down block. At the time of the block, the face is directed to the front, the lower abdomen is flexed, and the left arm is fully straightened for a strong block. The body is over Line 1 in a right half-facing (hanmi) stance.

2. Pivoting on the left foot, advance along the left branch of Line 1 with the right foot. The left fist, which blocked in the preceding movement, is drawn back to the left hip, while the right fist is thrust outward to the middle level in a rotating motion until the palm is directed downward. This is the basic middle level front attack. As shown in figure 4, the body has assumed a front (zenkutsu) stance (the mirror image of stance 1) with the left leg fully straight-

---

3. The word *yōi* means "ready." The term *yame* at the end of a kata includes an implication of readiness. Since "ending ready" is a cumbersome expression, I will continue to use the Japanese terms *yōi* and *yame* to designate the ready positions at the beginning and end of the kata. [Translator's note.]

5   6   3   7   4   8   5

ened. Equal strength is to be applied simultaneously to the retracted and attacking fists. One should be facing along the left branch of Line 1, the chin drawn in slightly, and the lower abdomen flexed.

3. Pivoting clockwise on the left foot through 180 degrees, step onto the right branch of Line 1 with the right foot. During the turn, the right hand, which was used in the attack, blocks downward from above the left shoulder. One has assumed a front stance as shown in figure 6, with the fingers of the blocking right fist downward. This movement should be executed as a single, rapid unit.

4. Pivoting on the right foot, step along the right branch of Line 1 with the left foot at the same time executing a middle level front attack with the left fist and drawing the right fist back to a point above the right hip. The fingers of the retracted and cocked right fist are upward, those of the attacking left fist downward.

5. Pivoting again on the right foot, turn counterclockwise through 90 degrees and advance along Line 2 with the left foot, assuming a front stance. During the turn, block downward as shown in figure 8 from above the right shoulder with the left fist, which performed the middle level attack in Movement 4. It is important in turning that the weight not be placed on the toes of the pivot foot.

6. Pivoting on the left foot, advance along Line 2 with the right foot, at the same time drawing the left fist, which performed the block in the previous movement, back to a point above the left hip and executing a middle level front attack with the right fist in a rotating motion from the right hip. The stance is the front stance, with both legs equally tensed, shoulders down and the chest directed to the front, the face directed to the front, chin drawn in, and lower abdomen flexed.

7. Pivoting on the right foot, advance with the left foot along Line 2. As shown in figure 10, pull the right fist back to the hip from its attacking position while executing a left middle level front attack. The stance is the front stance.

8. Pivoting on the left foot, advance along Line 2 with the right foot, execut-

9	**6**	10	**7**

ing a middle level front attack with the right fist and drawing the left fist back to the left hip. At this point, one has executed three consecutive front attacks, two with the right fist and one with the left. He should apply particular strength in the third attack and give a *kiai*. Following the third attack, he should pause long enough to draw in breath rather than proceeding immediately into the next movement. Figure 11 is identical to figure 9, showing the right middle level front attack.

9. Pivoting on the right foot, turn counterclockwise through 270 degrees and advance along the right branch of Line 3, executing a left down block as shown in figure 13. This movement is similar to Movement 5, i.e., pivoting counterclockwise on the right foot, one brings the left fist downward from above the right shoulder to complete a block at the same instant that he brings the left foot into position. The left fist is stopped at a point about six to seven inches above the left knee. Draw the right fist, which performed the attack in the previous movement, back to the right hip. The eyes are directed along the right

13	**9**	14	**10**	15	16 **11**

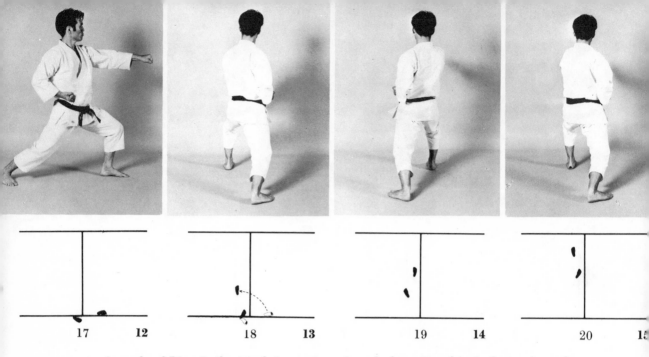

17 **12**	18 **13**	19 **14**	20 **15**

branch of Line 3, the trunk is erect, and, as before, the chin is drawn in and the lower abdomen flexed.

10. Pivoting on the left foot, advance one step with the right foot along the right branch of Line 3, executing a middle level front attack with the right fist and drawing the left fist as usual back to the left hip. The entire movement is to be performed in a continuous motion.

11. Pivoting clockwise through 180 degrees on the left foot, execute a right down block as shown in figure 16.

12. Advancing with the left foot along the left branch of Line 3, execute a left middle level front attack.

13. Pivoting counterclockwise through 90 degrees on the right foot, advance with the left foot along Line 2, executing a left down block while assuming a front stance.

14. Step forward with the right foot, execute a right middle level front attack.

21 **16**	22	23 **17**	24 **18**

25   26   **19**   27   **20**   28

15. Step forward with the left foot, execute a left middle level front attack.

16. Step forward with the right foot, execute a right middle level front attack with all one's strength and give a kiai. Following the attack, pause long enough to draw in breath before continuing to the next movement.

17. Pivoting counterclockwise through 270 degrees on the right foot, as in Movement 9, step onto the left branch of Line 1 and execute a left down block.

18. Advance to the front with the right foot and execute a right middle level front attack.

19. Pivoting clockwise through 180 degrees on the left foot, assume a front stance and execute a right down block.

20. Advance to the front one step with the left foot, executing a left middle level front attack.

Yame. Pivoting on the right foot, turn counterclockwise to return the left foot to its starting position on the left branch of Line 1. This is to be performed slowly and calmly, and it is very important that one not relax his alertness during the yame movement.

Execute the movements of the form lightly and correctly until the sequence is mastered, then apply strength to the motions. Moreover, it is important that the form be practiced repeatedly, so that one unconsciously executes each movement correctly.

The foregoing description refers to Taikyoku Shodan. The following modify these instructions to produce Taikyoku Nidan and Sandan:

The sequence of Taikyoku Nidan is identical to that of Shodan except that in Nidan, all punches are upper level instead of middle level attacks.

In Taikyoku Sandan, the down blocks along Lines 1 and 3 of Taikyoku Shodan are replaced with middle level arm blocks (*ude uke*) executed in back (kōkutsu) stance, and the threefold sets of middle level front attacks along Line 2 become sets of upper level attacks, the remaining movements being identical to Taikyoku Shodan.

The Taikyoku forms consist of units, with blocks followed by single front attacks along Lines 1 and 3, or blocks followed by three continuous front attacks along Line 2, each form having altogether twenty movements. If the twenty movements are to be executed correctly and smoothly, one must practice until these block-attack combinations can be performed in a single continuous motion of breathing and body movement. Through such practice, one will come to understand the three cardinal points of karate, i.e., the light and heavy application of strength, expansion and contraction of the body, and fast and slow techniques. By always practicing the kata seriously and visualizing realistically the opponents around oneself, one will gain insight into the concept that all the movements that shift the body in different directions are equivalent in a higher sense to a single transcendent movement involving the mind, weapon, and body as a unit. Related to this, one will come to understand the statement, "There is no *sente* [first attack] in karate," the state of absolute passiveness. It is because of these properties that the name Taikyoku has been assigned to these forms.

HEIAN SHODAN

There are twenty-one movements in this form, to be completed in about one minute. The line of movement is of the I category.

Yōi. Bow as directed in the discussion of Taikyoku Shodan. The readiness stance is that shown in figure 1. The first movement, which is made on a command from the leader in the case of group practice, is made from this stance. In training alone, the student should count the movements to himself.

1. Facing to the left, advance the left foot one step to the left along Line 1, and sweep to the left in a left downward block, as shown in figure 2.

2. Then, simultaneously step forward with the right foot along Line 1 and attack with the right fist to the middle level (figure 3).

3. Withdraw the right leg to the right branch of Line 1 and sweep downward

1   2 1   3 2   4 3

5   6   7   8   4

in a right down block (figure 4) assuming as the stance the mirror image of that of Movement 1.

4. Simultaneously draw back the right leg and fist. In this motion, describe a large arc with the right fist, passing in front of the left shoulder, continuing in front of the forehead, and stopping with the arm extended at the level of the shoulder (figure 8). The right leg is drawn back and straightened. It should he noted that the intent here is to free the wrist from an opponent's grasp following the block to the right and to attack his face or forearm.

5. As shown in figure 9, step forward along the right branch of Line 1 with the left leg and attack to the middle level with the left fist, simultaneously withdrawing the right fist to the hip. (This is the mirror image of the motion shown in figure 3.)

6. Pivoting on the right foot, take one step forward along Line 2, and execute a down block from a front stance (figure 10).

7. Open the left hand and raise it to a position in front of the forehead, as

9   5   10   6, 7   11   12

13   14   15   8   16

shown in figure 12. At the completion of the movement, the left elbow should be slightly bent, and the distance between the back of the raised hand and the forehead should be about six to seven inches.

The opponent, finding his attack to the lower level blocked, suddenly attacks the face with his right fist; this is the attack being blocked with the left wrist here.

8. Step forward with the right foot along Line 2 and straighten the legs.[4] At the same time, first touch the left elbow with the back of the right fist, turning the back of the left fist toward the front, and then, crossing the wrists, pull the left hand back to the hip and bring the right fist up to the forehead in a blocking position.

Following a block by the left hand of the opponent's right fist attack, the point here is to grasp the opponent's right wrist with the left hand and, twisting the grasped wrist in an outward direction, to break the opponent's right elbow by bringing the right forearm up against it. However, the eighth movement may also be used as a block against an upper level attack. After becoming accustomed to the seventh and eighth movements, one should execute them together as a single movement.

9. Step forward with the left foot along Line 2. Simultaneously, while opening the right hand, which was brought up in front of the forehead, and rotating it so that the palm is facing to the back, bring the back of the left fist against the right elbow and then, crossing the wrists, draw the right fist down to the hip, and bring the left fist up to the forehead as shown in figure 17. This is exactly the mirror image of the eighth movement. Note that the meaning of this movement is identical to that of the eighth movement and should be studied as such.

10. This is the same as Movement 8 (figure 15). Perform a kiai at the final moment of the motion of bringing the fist above the forehead.

---

4. Customarily the front stance is used in Movements 8, 9 and 10, as shown in figures 16, 18 and 20. [Translator's note.]

50   THE KATA

17   **9**   18   19   **10**   20

11. Pivoting counterclockwise on the right foot, step out along the right branch of Line 3 with the left foot and perform a left down block. This is similar to Movement 1.

12. Step forward along the right branch of Line 3 with the right foot and simultaneously execute a middle level front attack with the right fist.

13. Pivoting clockwise on the left foot, return the right foot toward the left branch of Line 3 and execute a down block movement from a front stance.

14. Step forward with the left foot onto the left branch of Line 3 and execute a middle level front attack with the left fist.

The meaning of this movement is identical to that of Movement 5. In this case, as in all others, be careful to have the feet turn inward with a feeling of forcing them together. It is of course very important to have the hips low and firmly set.

15. Pivoting counterclockwise on the right foot, step forward along Line 2 and execute a left down block from a front stance.

21   **11**   22   **12**   23   **13**   24   **14**

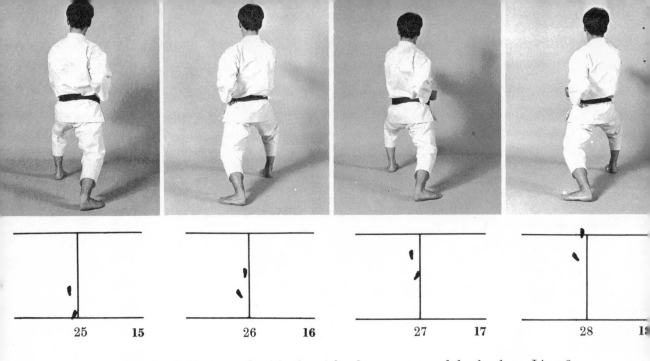

25 **15**   26 **16**   27 **17**   28 1[

16. Stepping forward with the right foot to proceed back along Line 2, execute a middle level front attack with the right fist.

17. Stepping forward with the left foot, execute a left middle level front attack. Note that whenever the same technique is performed three times in sequence, as in the present case, there should be some variation in strength of execution, with a feeling of application of greater force in the first and third movements and less, relatively, in the second.

18. Continue by taking another step forward along Line 2 with the right foot (front stance) and execute the middle level front attack with the right fist.

Apply more strength here than in either Movements 16 or 17 and make the step with a feeling of a broader and firmer base. At the moment of focus, perform a kiai.

19. Pivoting counterclockwise on the right foot, step forward along the left branch of Line 1 into a back (kōkutsu) stance; opening both hands, bring the left sword hand (shutō) to the front of the right shoulder and then extend it

29   30 **19**   31 **20**   32 2

33　　22　　　　　34

forward as if sliding it along the right arm, simultaneously drawing the right hand diagonally back to the position shown in figure 30. This is the left middle level sword hand block (chūdan shutō-uke).

This is the most difficult technique of Heian Shodan and must therefore be practiced very carefully. Assuming the back (kōkutsu) stance, hold the body in a half-facing (hanmi) posture with the face turned in the direction of the extended hand and foot. Bend the left elbow slightly, so that the distance between it and the side of the body is six to seven inches and the tip of the left index finger is about at the level of the left shoulder, and bend the thumb inward. The position of the right hand is intended to protect the trunk. It should be held horizontally at about the level of the solar plexus with the fingertips about even with the side of the body. The thumb should be bent here also.

20. Pivoting on the left foot, step toward the front with the right foot moving diagonally away from the left branch of Line 1 (back stance). At the same time, in the mirror image of Movement 19, extend the right hand in front of the right shoulder, holding the elbow slightly bent. The left hand is held in a horizontal position in front of the solar plexus as a protection for the trunk region.

This movement is a block with the right wrist against an attack. Following it, seek an opening, grasp the opponent's wrist with the right hand and, pulling him inward, attack his solar plexus with a left spear hand (nukite). Movements 19, 21 and 22 have a similar meaning.

21. Pivoting on the left foot, step onto the right branch of Line 1, assuming a back stance. Extend the right hand in front of the right shoulder, hold the left hand in a horizontal position across the solar plexus, and face to the right, sighting along the right hand.

At this time, pay particular attention to the legs. Supporting the weight on the rear leg, hold the front foot on the ground with the feeling of pulling slightly back against the friction of the gently resting toes.

22. Step forward with the left foot, moving diagonally away from the right branch of Line 1, into a back stance and execute a left middle level sword hand block.

HEIAN SHODAN   53

This completes the Heian Shodan form. Since Movements 7 and 8 are properly a single movement, the form consists in fact of only twenty-one movements.

Yame. At the command "Yame," withdraw the left foot to Line 1, form fists with both hands, and return to a stance similar to that of yōi. The yame stance should be assumed calmly and without haste. Note that the starting and finishing points, the positions of yōi and yame, should always occur at the same spot on the floor.

HEIAN NIDAN

At one time, this form was Heian Shodan. There are twenty-six movements to be completed in about one minute. The comments in the discussion of Heian Shodan concerning counting, the bows, and yōi apply here as well. The line of movement is of the I type as in Heian Shodan.

1. Stepping with the left foot along the left branch of Line 1, holding the right foot in place and assuming a back stance, raise both fists to the positions shown in figure 2. The trunk is directed forward, while the face is turned to the left.

With this movement, one blocks an attack to the face from the left with the left wrist and protects the head with the right fist, which is set for attack.

2. Without changing the position of the feet, pull the left fist inward to a position in front of the right shoulder and attack to the left with the right hand in a wide circular motion. The trunk is twisted sideways to face to the left. Note that this movement is performed with the feeling of pulling the opponent in with the left hand and attacking sideways with the right fist (i.e., hammer fist).

1   2   **1–3**   3   4

5 **4–6**   6   7

3. Without shifting the feet,[5] attack in a horizontal line to the left side with the left fist (fingers downward), at the same time pulling the right fist to the side at a point above the hip.

Following the attack with the right fist, attack immediately, without the slightest pause, with the left fist, paying particular attention to the movement of the hips.

4. Looking to the right along Line 1, bring the right fist to a position off the right shoulder with the elbow bent and the fingers to the front, and bring the left fist to a point in front of the head one or two inches from the forehead. This is the mirror image of the stance shown in figure 2.

5. Without changing the position of the feet, simultaneously pull the right fist to a point in front of the left shoulder and attack with the left fist to the right side, describing a large arc with the fist.

6. Without altering the stance,[6] simultaneously extend the right fist horizontally to the right and pull the left fist to the left hip. This is the mirror image of the movement shown in figure 4.

7. Draw the left foot a half step toward the right and, as illustrated in figure 8, simultaneously look to the rear, draw the sole of the right foot up beside the left knee, and rest the right fist on the left fist with the fingers of the right fist toward the body.

8. Standing with the left leg slightly bent, attack simultaneously the opponent's face with the right back fist (uraken) and his groin or chest with the right sword foot (sokutō). Note that one should execute Movements 7 and 8 as a single movement after becoming familiar with the techniques. In this movement, simultaneous fist and foot attacks are being made as one turns to face an opponent sensed (during Movement 6) to be attacking from behind.

9. While lowering the kicking foot to the base of Line 1, face forward along

5. In the latest edition, this stance is the immovable (*fudō-dachi*). [Translator's note.]
6. In the latest edition, this stance is the immovable (*fudō-dachi*). [Translator's note.]

8   **7, 8**   9   10   11

Line 2, assume a back stance, and execute a left sword hand block (cf. Heian Shodan, Movements 19 and 22).

10. Step forward with the right foot along Line 2 and assume the left back stance, at the same time executing a right sword hand block (cf. Heian Shodan, Movements 20 and 21).

11. Step forward with the left foot along Line 2 and assume the right back stance, at the same time executing a left sword hand block. This movement is similar to Movement 9 (cf. Movements 19 and 22 of Heian Shodan).

12. Step forward one step with the right foot standing with both legs straightened,[7] and execute a middle level attack with the right four-finger spear hand (shihon-nukite) with the back of the extended right hand to the right; at the same time slide the back of the open left hand along the undersurface of the right arm up to the armpit.

While deflecting an opponent's attack downward and drawing it in with the palm of the left hand, one makes a spear hand (nukite) attack to the solar plexus. The motions of the hands and feet are coordinated. Give a kiai at the moment of focus (*kime*).

13. Pivoting counterclockwise on the right foot, turn to the left to assume a right back stance with the left foot on the right branch of Line 3 and execute a left sword hand block. Note that this movement is similar to Movement 19 of Heian Shodan.

14. Keeping the left foot in place step diagonally to the front, i.e., to a position between the right branches of Lines 1 and 3, assume a back stance, and execute a right sword hand block. Note that this movement is similar to Movement 20 of Heian Shodan.

15. Continuing to keep the left foot in place, shift the right foot to the left branch of Line 3, assume a back stance, and execute a right sword hand block. This movement is similar to the preceding one. It is also similar to Movement 21 of Heian Shodan.

---

7. Customarily this movement is performed with the front stance. [Translator's note.]

56   THE KATA

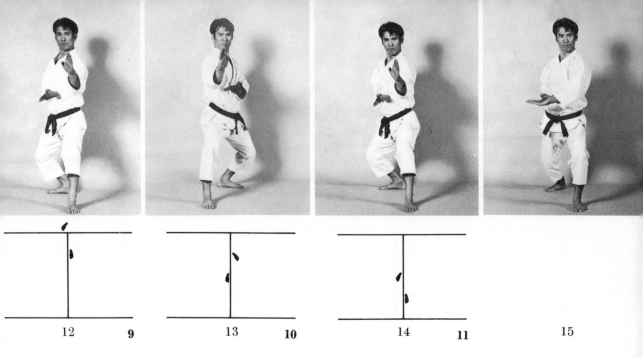

9   12   10   13   11   14   15

16. Keeping the right foot in place, simultaneously step diagonally to the front with the left foot and execute a left sword hand block. This is similar to Movement 22 of Heian Shodan.

17. Keeping the right foot in place and shifting the left foot to Line 2, simultaneously draw the left hand, the fist clenched with the fingers upward, back to the hip and execute a right middle level block, swinging the fist, fingers to the back, in a wide circular motion from a position in which the arm is extended downward and slanting outward to one bringing the fist past the left shoulder to execute the block.

The right shoulder is directed to the front and the left shoulder drawn back. The heel of the back foot has a tendency to rise, but one should take care that it remains firmly planted.

The point in this block is to snag-block an opponent's attack to the chest with one's right wrist. This block is called the forearm block (uchi-uke).

18. Keeping the left foot in place, and without altering the position of the

16   12   17   13   18   14   19   15

20   **16**   21   **17**   22   23

arms, kick upward with the right foot as high as possible in front of the right fist.

The point here is to grasp an opponent's left wrist and to kick his elbow with the right foot. One should practice kicking as high as possible.

19. Lowering the kicking foot to a position on Line 2, simultaneously withdraw the right fist to the right hip, fingers upward, and execute a middle level reverse punch with the left fist.

20. Without shifting the feet, execute a left middle level forearm block, describing a counterclockwise arc in front of the body with the left fist. This movement is the mirror image of Movement 17.

One should be careful to have the left shoulder toward the front and the right drawn back toward the rear, as well as to hold the back heel fixed.

21. Without shifting the right foot or the positions of the two arms, kick high to the front with the left feet. This is the mirror image of Movement 18.

22. While lowering the left kicking foot to a position on Line 2, withdraw the

24   25   26   **18**   27

28   **19**   29

30   **20**   31   32   33   **21**

left fist and attack with a right middle level reverse punch. This is the mirror image of Movement 19.

23. Without moving the left foot, take a large forward step with the right foot (along Line 2). Assuming a front stance,[8] execute a middle level double hand block with the right fist, fingers upward, at the same time bringing the left fist up to touch the right elbow. This block is called *morote-uke*. For the middle level block, the elbow should be slightly bent and six to seven inches from the side of the body, as in the sword hand block (shutō-uke).

---

8. In the latest edition, this stance is the immovable (*fudō-dachi*). [Translator's note.]

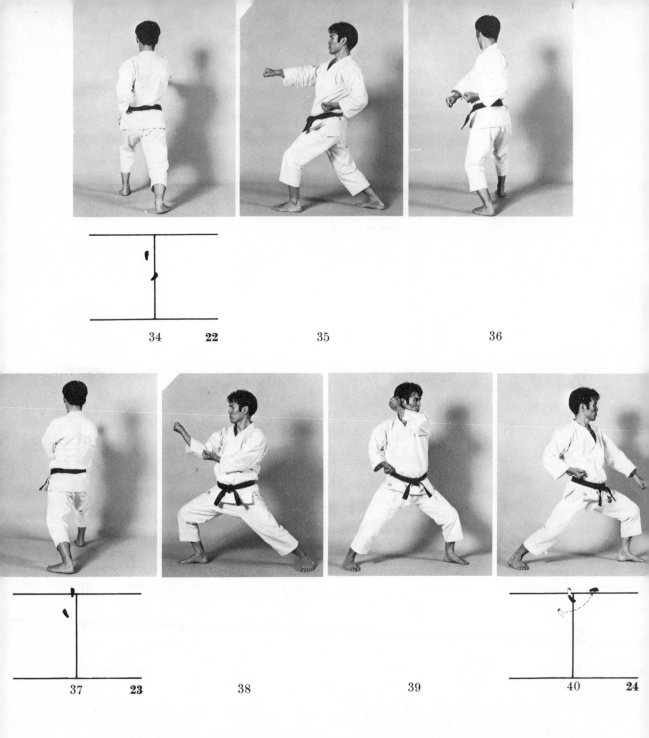

34   **22**   35   36

37   **23**   38   39   40   **24**

24. Pivoting counterclockwise on the right foot, turn to the left, placing the left foot on the left branch of Line 1, assume a front stance, and simultaneously bring the right fist to the hip and execute a down block with the left fist. This is similar to Movement 1 of Heian Shodan.

25. Without moving the left foot, open the left hand and bring it to the forehead, at the same time stepping to the right, with the right foot, diagonally away from the left branch of Line 1. Straighten the legs and execute an upper

41   42   43   44 **25**

45 **26**   46 **27**   47   48

level block with the right fist with the fingers directed to the front and withdraw the left fist to the hip.[9]

This is similar to Movements 7 and 8 of Heian Shodan. As in Movement 7 in that kata, first open the left fist and raise it to a position in front of and above the forehead, then slide the back of the right fist past the left elbow with the two wrists crossing.

26. Without shifting the left foot, move the right foot to Line 1 and, while

---

9. In the latest edition, this stance is the front stance. [Translator's note.]

assuming a front stance, execute a down block with the right fist and withdraw the left fist to the hip. This motion is similar to Movement 3 of Heian Shodan.

27. Keeping the right foot in place, the left foot steps out (diagonally right front) midway between the right branch of Line 1 and Line 2. While straightening the legs, open the right fist, which was in the lower level blocking position, raise it above the head, and draw it back to the hip as if grasping and twisting the enemy's arm; raise the left fist to a position above the head. The movements of both wrists, which cross, are as I have mentioned before. This time, at the moment of impact emit a kiai (*kakegoe*). (NB: the customary front stance is shown in figure 47.)

Yame. With this movement, the kata is completed. At the command of yame, draw the left foot inward and slowly assume the original yōi stance.

In this description, there are twenty-seven movements in the kata; however, since Movements 7 and 8 are to be executed as a single motion, there are in fact twenty-six movements.

HEIAN SANDAN

There are altogether twenty-three movements in this form, taking about one minute to complete. The comments about commands, bows, and so on are the same as those for Heian Shodan. The line of movement is of the T form.

Yōi. As in Heian Shodan, the stance here is the natural open V stance. Both arms are held in a natural position in front of the thighs. This yōi stance is shown in figure 1.

1. Without moving the right foot, step out along the left branch of Line 1 with the left foot and assume the right back stance. In a ripping motion of the fists, move the right fist from in front of the left shoulder and the left fist from the thigh, blocking as shown in figure 3 with the left fist. The trunk is in a half-facing posture and the face turned in the direction of the left fist. The

1   2   3   **1**   4   2,

5 6 7 8 4

purpose here is to block an attack to the left rib cage by an opponent from the left.

2. Keeping the left foot in place, bring the right foot up to the left and assume a feet-together (heisoku) stance. Facing toward the left, switch blocking hands, pulling the two fists in opposite directions, bringing the right fist, from below, outside the left elbow and up, and swinging the left fist downward from the right shoulder. Thus, the right arm executes a middle level block, and the left arm swings downward in a lower level block. Refer to figure 4.

At the end of the motion, the right arm is half bent and the right elbow about six inches from the chest with the right fist about at the level of the shoulder. The fists are about a shoulder's width apart. The opponent, finding his right fist attack blocked in Movement 1, now attacks with his left fist and foot: the point here is to block these two attacks.

3. Without altering the stance, bring the right fist down, passing inside the left elbow, and the left fist up, passing outside the right elbow, in a ripping motion, to execute a lower level block with the right fist and a middle level block with the left. This movement is the mirror image of that shown in figure 4.

Withdrawing his fist and foot after the preceding blocks, the opponent now attacks with the opposite fist and foot. The point of the present movement is to block the right fist attack with the left arm and to deflect the foot attack downward with the right fist. Movements 2 and 3 are blocks against combined fist and foot attacks from the left side and can turn a disadvantageous position into a favorable one. It should be noted that in actual practice, the lower setting of the front stance would be preferable to the one here against an opponent's combined attack.

4. Pivoting clockwise on the left foot, bring the right foot toward the right branch of Line 1 into a left back stance. Simultaneously pull the left fist back to the hip, passing in front of the right shoulder, and swing the right fist from

9   10   **5, 6**   11   12

outside the left elbow to execute a middle level block to the right side. Face in the direction of the right fist, holding the body in a half-facing posture. This position is the mirror image of that shown in figure 3.

5. Keeping the right foot in place and drawing the left foot to it, assume a feet-together (heisoku) stance and execute simultaneously a middle level block with the left arm and a lower level block with the right. This is the mirror image of Movement 2.

6. Without altering the stance, switch blocking hands, executing a middle level block with the right fist and a lower level block with the left. This is the mirror image of Movement 3.

7. Without moving the right foot, simultaneously step with the left foot along Line 2 into a right back stance and execute a left double hand block (morote-uke), bringing the right fist, with the fingers upward, up beside the left elbow.

8. Keeping the left foot in place and stepping with the right foot along Line

13   **7**   14   15

16   8   17   18

2, bring the left sword hand down to a point under the right upper arm, palm downward, and execute a right middle level four-finger spear hand (shihon nukite) attack with the palm turned toward the left side. The right hand is thrust forward from a point just above the wrist of the left sword hand. The meaning here is that the left palm is to depress and draw in the wrist of an opponent's right fist as it attacks the chest, while the right four-finger spear hand is a counterattack to the opponent's solar plexus.

9. Rotate the spear hand to the left as shown in figure 18. Pivoting on the right foot, turn the whole body counterclockwise 180 degrees to the left, stepping forward with the left foot along Line 2 to assume a horse-riding stance. During the turn, straighten the left arm to perform a left iron hammer (tettsui) attack to the side, fingers downward, pulling the right fist back to the hip and turning the face to the left (looking along Line 2).

Dropping the hips, extend the left iron hammer (hit with the little finger side of the fist) level with the shoulder. The opponent has blocked the four-finger

19   20   9   21   10   22   11

23   24   25   **12–14**   26

spear thrust and grasped and twisted the wrist to the left, so the intent here is to turn one's body with the twist, turning to the left so that the wrist is to the back and attacking with an iron hammer to the opponent's side.

10. Keeping the left foot in place and taking a large step forward along Line 2 into a front stance, simultaneously draw the left fist back to the hip and execute a middle level attack with the right fist.

The opponent having fallen back in surprise, one takes the advantage and executes a finishing attack to his solar plexus. Give a kiai at this point.

11. Without shifting the right foot, draw the left foot in to the right and turn counterclockwise through half a revolution so as to face to the rear along Line 2 in a feet-together stance, at the same time resting both fists above the hips with the fingers to the back and the elbows akimbo.

Apply full strength with a kiai in Movement 10; then execute Movement 11 slowly. This is an example of two of the cardinal points of the kata, the degree of strength and fast and slow techniques, as described earlier.

12. Keeping the left foot as it is and without breaking the posture of the upper body, bring the right knee up high, swing the right elbow back slightly, and while stamping down back along Line 2 execute a right elbow (*empi*) technique with the fists still resting on the hips. Continue looking towards the opponent along Line 2. The stance at this time is horse riding.

The intent here is to stamp on and break the opponent's thigh and at the same time attack the solar plexus with the right elbow. In a real situation it is awkward to have both fists resting on the hips, so an opponent's right fist attack is blocked with the left fist; then grasping the wrist, pull the opponent in and attack his chest with the right elbow. Immediately follow up with a back fist attack to the opponent's philtrum (*jinchū*).

13. Without altering the position of the feet or the posture, attack to the side with the right fist, bringing the fist up in a circular motion in front of the right shoulder and then out (toward the back of Line 2), keeping the elbow slightly bent, the fist about level with the shoulder, and the back of the fist turned

66 THE KATA

27   28   29

downward. Note that as described in the preceding step the point here is an attack to the opponent's philtrum with the back fist strike.

14. Without altering the position of the feet or the posture, return the right fist to its position above the right hip with the fingers to the back. Movements 13 and 14 are to be performed in rapid succession.

15. Keeping the right foot in place and without altering the posture, simultaneously stamp forward with the left foot along Line 2 and execute a left elbow attack. This movement is the mirror image of Movement 12.

16. Without altering the posture, swing the left fist up past the left shoulder and down with the fingers upward. The motion of the fist should end at about the level of the shoulder, this movement being the mirror image of Movement 13.

17. Without altering the posture, return the left fist to the hip with the fingers to the back in a motion that is the mirror image of Movement 14.

18. As in Movement 12, keeping the left foot in place and without altering

30   31   32   33

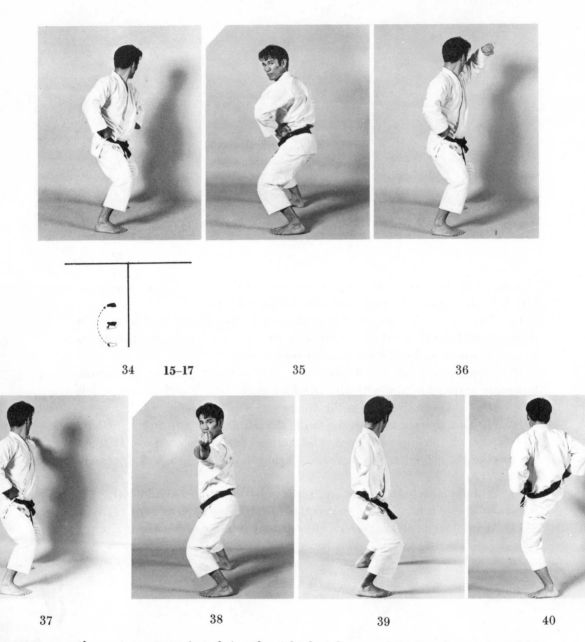

34   **15–17**   35   36

37   38   39   40

the posture, stamp in to bring the right foot down on Line 2 and execute a right elbow attack.

19. Without altering the stance, attack to the right with the right back fist. This is the same as Movement 13.

20. Without altering the stance, return the right fist to the right hip. This is the same as Movement 14. Note that Movements 12 through 20 in this kata are a threefold repetition of a technique. There are many instances of this in the different kata, and in all such cases, the second movement is executed relatively lightly and the third with great strength.

68   THE KATA

41 **18–20**   42   43   44

45 **21**   46   47   48

21. Without shifting the right foot, step toward the starting position along Line 2 assuming a front stance and facing toward the starting position and execute a left middle level attack, with the right fist at the hip, fingers upward.[10]

22. Without shifting the left foot, draw the right foot up to the left into a position with both feet on Line 1 and slightly separated, and then without pausing pivot counterclockwise 180 degrees to the left on the right foot. As the

10. At the present time, it is customary at the start of this movement to extend the right arm out to the side, i.e., toward the starting point of Line 2, as if grasping an opponent's lapel and pulling it inward. [Translator's note.]

49	50	51
22	**23**	

left foot is again placed on Line 1 (horse-riding stance), swing the right fist up, with elbow bent and fingers inward, in a sweeping motion to a point over the left shoulder, and thrust the left elbow out toward the back keeping the left fist clenched. Continue to face directly forward. The final position is the mirror image of that shown in figure 50.

The purpose of this motion is to escape encirclement of the body by an opponent's arms from behind. One lowers the hips and simultaneously attacks the face with his right fist and the side with his left elbow.

23. Without altering the horse-riding stance, shift to the right (*yori-ashi*), swinging the left fist up to a point above the right shoulder and thrusting the right elbow to the back.[11] This is the motion shown in figure 50. The movement is the mirror image of Movement 22.

Yori-ashi consists of tensing the left foot, for example, and pushing off with it to slide both feet to the right so that one shifts his position without altering his stance. As in Movements 22 and 23, there are many instances in the various kata in which a technique is executed first to one side, then to the other. One must always keep in mind that the purpose is not only to maintain a balance of motions but also to develop spontaneity of movement, to the left and right, to the front and back, that is required in proper defensive response to a critical situation.

Yame. Keeping the left foot in place, draw the right foot part of the way in toward it, straighten the knees, and lower both fists to positions in front of the thighs to return to the yōi stance.

---

11. Customarily there is a kiai at this point in the kata. [Translator's note.]

HEIAN YODAN

There is a total of twenty-seven movements in this form, which takes about one minute to complete. The line of movement is of the plus-minus type.

Yōi. The stance is the same as that in Heian Shodan.

1. Without moving the right foot, step with the left foot along Line 1 and assume a right back stance. At the same time, open the fists, holding the four fingers together and the thumb bent, and bring the right arm up in front of the forehead, with the elbow bent and the back of the hand toward the forehead, while simultaneously holding the left arm out to the left with the forearm vertical, the elbow bent, and the palm turned toward the right (i.e., in the same direction as the chest). The face is turned to the left.[12]

This stance is similar to that of Heian Nidan shown on page 54 except that the hands are open. The point here is almost the same as that of the first movement of Heian Nidan, that is, to block and grasp an opponent's wrist with the left hand in preparation for pulling him inward and attacking his philtrum or the side of his neck with the right sword hand.

2. Pivoting to the right with the feet in place, assume a left back stance. At the same time turn the head to face to the right, bring the right hand, with fingers together, to an upper level position, and bring the back of the left hand to the forehead.[13] This is the mirror image of Movement 1.

3. Without moving the right foot while stepping forward with the left (front stance) cross the wrists without bending them, with the right fist above; thrust forward into the lower section keeping the upper body upright, face forward.

Straighten both elbows; both fists should be about seven to eight inches away

---

12. This movement is customarily performed slowly. [Translator's note.]

13. It is customary to move the arms as shown in figure 3 before executing the double arm block in Movement 2. [Translator's note.]

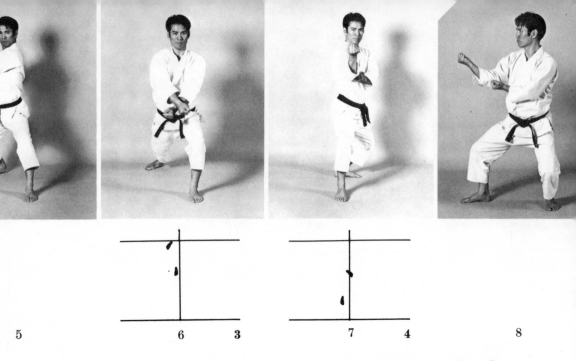

5   6   3   7   4   8

from the body. The intent here is to block an opponent's kicking attack to the groin with the fist against the opponent's shin. Therefore, the upper body should not lean forward nor should the line of vision be lowered.

4. Keeping the left foot in place, simultaneously step forward with the right foot into a back stance along Line 2 and execute a middle level block with the right fist, fingers upward, the left fist being held lightly against the inside of the right elbow with the back of the fist downward.

5. Without moving the right foot, draw the left foot toward the right and turn the head to face to the left. At the same time, pull the right fist, with the fingers upward, back to the right hip, place the left fist on it with the fingers toward the back, and slide the sole of the left foot up to a point above the inside of the right knee. This is the mirror image of the movement of Heian Nidan shown on page 56.

6. Standing on the right foot, attack to the left simultaneously with a left back fist and a left sword foot (sokutō). This is the mirror image of the move-

9   5, 6   10   11   7   12

13   8, 9   14   15   10   16

ment of Heian Nidan shown on page 56. Note that sword foot (sokutō) refers to the outside edge of the foot. For the meaning of this movement, refer to the explanation of Movements 7 and 8 of Heian Nidan.

7. Placing the left foot down on Line 3 in a front stance, execute a right elbow attack to the front, the fingers of the right fist downward, with the right forearm about six to seven inches from the chest, striking the right elbow with the palm of the left hand (see figure 11).

Immediately following the attack to the opponent's philtrum with the left back fist and to his side or testicles with the left sword foot, step in toward him with the left foot, grasp his arm to pull him inward, and attack with the right elbow.

8. Without moving the left foot, draw the right foot in toward the left and bring it up to a point above the inside of the left knee; then simultaneously turn the head to face to the right side, pull the left fist back to the left hip, fingers upward, and place the right fist on top of it with the fingers toward the body. This is the same stance as that of Heian Nidan shown on page 56.

9. Continuing to stand on the left foot and looking to the right side, attack simultaneously with the right sword foot and the right back fist. This is the same motion as that of Heian Nidan shown on page 56.

10. Lowering the right foot onto the right branch of Line 3 in a front stance, execute a left elbow attack, striking the outside of the left elbow with the right hand. This is the mirror image of Movement 7. The final stance is that shown in figure 15.

11. Keeping the feet in place, turn the body to the front and straighten the legs.[14] While turning, bring the open right hand through a wide clockwise arc up past and almost touching the forehead, straighten the elbow, and execute an upper level right sword hand attack to the front. At the same time, execute a

---

14. Originally the stance was natural; now the front stance is customarily used. [Translator's note.]

17   18   11   19

20   12   21   22   23

left open hand rising block.[15] The posture from the waist up is that shown in figure 18. The purpose of the initial motion of the right hand toward the forehead is to catch the wrist of an opponent's attacking arm in the front with the right hand.

   12. Without altering the posture, kick as high as possible with the right foot,

---

15. It is currently the practice that the left hand be brought downward across the lower abdomen in a sweeping block before execution of the rising block described here. [Translator's note.]

16. It seems that the attacker's hand should be held by one's left hand. [Translator's note.]

24   13   25   26   27   14

aiming at the tip of the right hand, as shown in figure 20. The purpose of this technique is to break the elbow of an opponent's attacking arm with a kick while holding and drawing the arm in with the right hand.[16] The kicking foot must be withdrawn as quickly as possible.

13. Take a leaping step forward with the right foot, bringing the left foot to rest lightly on the ball of the foot at a point just behind the right foot, as shown in figure 24. At the same time, while first extending the left hand away from the forehead toward the front (as if stretching it out to grasp something) and then withdrawing it to the left hip, in a continuous motion draw the right fist inward and swing it out again in a back fist (uraken) attack to the front. Give a kiai, "Ei," at the moment of focus of this technique.

14. Pivoting to the left on the right foot, step with the left foot diagonally between Line 2 and the right branch of Line 3 (back stance). At the same time, cross the arms at the wrists, with the right closer to the body and the fingers toward the body, and immediately force them apart to the sides in an opening

28   15   29   30   16, 17   31

32   33   34   35   18

(*kakiwake*) motion, turning the fingers to the front at the end of the motion. The point here is to break apart a double fist (*morote-zuki*) attack, forcing the attacking arms to the two sides with the wrists; the wrists should be about a shoulder's width apart, and the elbows slightly bent. The stance should be that shown in figure 27.

15. Without altering the posture or the position of the left foot, kick high between the two fists with the right foot, as shown in figure 28.

16. As the right (kicking) foot touches the ground (front stance), execute a middle level attack with the right fist and pull the left fist to the hip. In this motion, do not pull the right fist back before the attack, but start the attack with it in the position described in Movement 15. To this end, hold the elbows slightly bent during Movements 14 and 15.

17. Without altering the stance, execute a left middle level reverse punch, pulling the right fist back to the hip. Movements 16 and 17 are to be executed in rapid succession once one has become used to them. The double movement is called continuous punching (*renzuki*).

36   19   37   **20, 21**   38   39

40 **22**	41	42 **23**	43 **24**

18. Pivoting on the left foot, step with the right foot diagonally between Line 2 and the left branch of Line 3 into a back stance. At the same time, cross the arms, with the right closer to the body, and immediately follow with the opening block. This movement is the mirror image of Movement 14.

19. Without moving the right foot or the body, kick high between the two fists with the left foot.

20. As the left foot touches the ground (front stance), execute a middle level attack with the left fist and pull the right fist back to the hip. Be sure to start the attack with the left fist from its position in the preceding movement.

21. Without altering the stance, simultaneously execute a right middle level reverse punch and pull the left fist back to the hip. Here again, as soon as the kicking foot touches the ground in Movement 20, attack with the left and right fists in rapid succession. This is the same as in Movements 16 and 17.

22. Without moving the right foot, step with the left foot diagonally to the left along Line 2 into a right back stance, simultaneously executing a middle level double hand block (morote-uke). The fingers of both fists face upward. This is identical to Movement 7 in Heian Sandan. Note that the body is directed to the right and the face to the front, i.e., toward Line 1. The left fist is in the position of a middle level block to the front. The right fist is held touching the left elbow.

23. Without moving the left foot, step forward along Line 2 toward Line 1, at the same time executing a middle level double hand block. This is the mirror image of Movement 22.

24. Without shifting the right foot, step forward with the left foot along Line 2 toward Line 1, at the same time executing a middle level double hand block. This is identical to Movement 22.

25. Extend the hands far to the front above the level of the head, with palms facing each other. Standing on the left foot, immediately bring the right knee up high and pull the clenched fists down to either side of the raised knee as

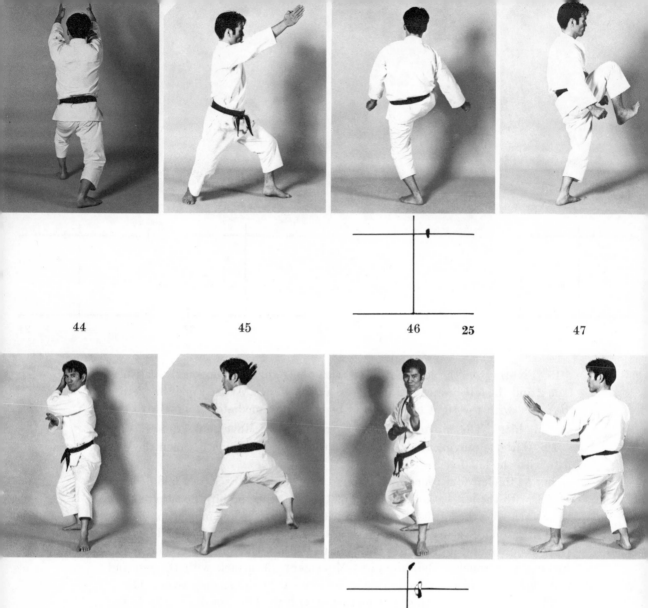

44 45 46 **25** 47

48 49 50 **26** 51

shown in figure 46. The purpose here is to crush the opponent's face, grasping the head and forcing it down onto the knee. Give a kiai at this point, "Ei!"

26. As soon as the right foot is lowered to the ground, turn to face to the rear, turning to the left without shifting either foot, and assuming a right back stance, and execute a left sword hand block. Rest the right sword hand against the solar plexus with the palm upward. This is the same stance as that of Heian Shodan shown on page 52.

27. Without moving the left foot, step forward with the right foot along Line 2 into a left back stance, at the same time executing a right sword hand block. This is the mirror image of Movement 26.

78 THE KATA

52   27   53   54

Yame. Without moving the left foot, draw the right foot back and assume the natural stance of yōi.

HEIAN GODAN

There are twenty-five movements in the form, which takes about one minute to complete. The line of movement is of the T category.

1. Without moving the right foot, assume a back stance with the left foot on the left branch of Line 1. At the same time, look to the left and execute a middle level forearm block with the left fist, fingers upward, pulling the right fist to the right hip. This is identical to the movement of Heian Sandan shown on page 62.

1   2   3   1, 2   4

2. Without changing the stance,[17] execute a reverse punch with the right fist and pull the left fist to the left hip. Twist the trunk to the left in executing the middle level attack. It is better to keep the right elbow bent slightly.

Block the opponent's fist from the left with a left forearm block (*uchi-uke*) and immediately grasp the opponent's wrist and thrust to the opponent's chest.

3. Without shifting the left foot, draw the right foot to the left into a feet-together (heisoku) stance. At the same time, turning the face to the right and pulling the right fist to the hip, set the left forearm horizontally about six inches in front of the chest with the fingers of the fist downward. Note that this movement is to be executed in an unhurried fashion, with the motions of the hand, foot, and face occurring simultaneously. Turn the eyes to the right as if following the movement of the left fist. The left fist is held in the water-flowing (*mizu-nagare*) position, with the forearm slanting slightly downward and the fist extending a short distance beyond the right side of the body, protecting the solar plexus.

4. Without shifting the left foot, assume a back stance, with the right foot on the right branch of Line 1. At the same time, look to the right and execute a middle level forearm block with the right fist, pulling the left fist back to the hip. This is the mirror image of Movement 1 and the same as Movement 4 of Heian Sandan. Since both Movements 1 and 4 require an initial motion to provide momentum to the fists, one precedes the middle level blocks with a crossing of the fists as in Heian Sandan.

5. Without changing the stance,[18] execute a left reverse punch, pulling the right fist back to the hip. The middle level attack is performed with a feeling of rotating the trunk. It is better to keep the left elbow bent slightly.

6. Without shifting the right foot, draw the left foot up to it into a feet-together stance, turning the face to the front. At the same time, pull the left fist back to the hip and position the right forearm horizontally in front of the chest.

17. In the latest edition, this stance is the immovable (*fudō-dachi*). [Translator's note.]
18. In the latest edition, this stance is the immovable (*fudō-dachi*). [Translator's note.]

9   **6**   10   11   **7**   12

7. Without shifting the left foot, step forward with the right foot onto Line 2 into a back stance. At the same time, execute a right middle level forearm block and place the left fist against the inside of the right elbow, with the fingers of both fists upward. The body is set in a half-facing (hanmi) posture with the face to the front.

8. Without shifting the right foot, step forward along Line 2 with the left foot into a front stance. At the same time, cross the arms at the wrists, with the right fist above the left and set so that the backs of the fists form a right angle, and thrust them forward in a downward direction. Keep the body upright and look directly to the front.

This is similar to Movement 3 of Heian Yodan. Straighten both elbows with the fist slightly inside the left knee. This is the stance for blocking an opponent's lower level kick.

9. Without altering the lower abdomen or legs, and with the wrists still crossed, open the hands and thrust them up in front of the head as shown in figure 14. Move swiftly at this point.

13   **8–11**   14   15

16   17   18   19

The feeling here is that of having blocked a lower level attack and finding the opponent again attacking to the upper level, thrusting the second attack upward without the slightest pause between blocks. The ability to adjust one's defense freely in response to a situation is a special quality of karate. The term, "adjusting to opponents," is used to denote such responses.

10. Without altering the position of the abdomen or legs, alter the cross of the wrists: while continuing to hold them against each other with the inside of the wrists pressed together, rotate them successively through a position of palms facing each other and into one of the right palm turned upward fingers pointing to the front and the left palm turned downward fingers pointing to the side. With the wrists still crossed, draw them toward the right hip. The position is that shown in figure 18. This motion deflects downward an attack made by an opponent immediately following the preceding upper level cross block (*kosa-uke*).

20   21   22   **12**   23

24   **13, 14**   25   26

11. Without altering the lower abdomen or legs, attack to the front with the left fist and simultaneously pull the right fist back to the right hip.

12. Without shifting the left foot, step forward along Line 2 with the right foot (front stance) and simultaneously execute a right middle level attack. Pull the left fist back to the hip. In this movement, attack with a feeling of sufficient strength to deliver a finishing blow and perform a kiai.

13. Pivoting counterclockwise 180 degrees on the left foot, step with the right foot toward the starting point into a horse-riding stance (kiba-dachi), at the same time executing a right down block, with the left fist at the hip and the body directed to the front, i.e., to the right side of Line 2. The face is looking to the right toward the origin of Line 2.

14. Keeping the abdomen and legs fixed, face to the left, i.e., toward the far end of Line 2. At the same time, move the arms as if drawing a bow, pulling the right fist to the hip and extending the left arm straight out to the side with the hand open and the palm turned inward, i.e., toward the right side of Line 2.

27   28   29   **15**   30

31   **16**   32   33   **17**   34

The point here is to hook an opponent's middle level attack with the left wrist.

15. Without moving the left foot, swing the right foot forward in a crescent-like motion and kick the left palm, as shown in figure 29. The point here is to grasp an opponent's right wrist with the left hand, draw him inward, and kick him in the chest. For this reason, one should develop the habit during practice of kicking as high as possible and particularly of not lowering the left hand. This technique is called the crescent moon kick (*mikazuki-geri*).

16. Lowering the right foot onto the far end of Line 2 (horse-riding stance), strike the left palm with the right elbow with the fingers of the right fist turned toward the body and the right forearm held six to seven inches from the chest. The left palm should be in the same place it was at the end of Movement 14, and one should be facing to the front, i.e., the left of Line 2. The point here is to attack an opponent with the right elbow while pulling him inward with the left hand.

17. Keep the right foot in place, shift the full weight to the right leg and draw the left foot behind the right. At the same time, turn the head to the right, i.e., away from the origin of Line 2, and execute a right middle level forearm block to the right, with the left fist held just touching the right elbow.

Bend the right knee slightly. Both fists are held with the fingers turned upward. The point of this movement is to block a middle level attack from the right made while one is attacking a first opponent with the right elbow in Movement 16.

18. Without moving the right foot, face to the left, i.e., to the origin of Line 2, and extend both fists upward, with fingers upward, as shown in figure 35, and, at the same time, step to the left (toward the origin of Line 2) with the left leg, toes resting lightly on the ground (see figure 36). Support the entire weight on the slightly bent right leg. The body, contracted into itself in Movement 17, is now, in Movement 18, suddenly greatly expanded with a feeling of overwhelming an opponent. This illustrates one of the cardinal points of kata practice: expanding and contracting the body (*tai no shinshuku*).

84 THE KATA

35 **18** 36 37

38 **19** 39 40 **20** 41 **21**

19. Jumping off toward the origin of Line 2 with the right leg, spring as high and as far as possible, turning to the left in the air.[19] Land as shown in figure 38 with the right knee bent and the left foot drawn up just behind the right, with fists crossed, the right above the left, and execute a lower level block. The face is directed to the front, i.e., to the right of Line 2.

20. Facing to the right and straightening the left leg without shifting the foot, take a large step toward the origin of Line 2 with the right foot, and as-

19. Customarily there is a kiai at this point in the kata, just before jumping. [Translator's note.]

42   43   44

45   **22**   46   47

sume a front stance,[20] at the same time executing a right middle level forearm block with fingers upward and resting the left fist with fingers upward at the inside of the right elbow.

    21. Face to the left,[21] i.e., to the far end of Line 2, and at the same time thrust the right sword hand, with the palm upward, forward to a point above the left knee and draw the left sword hand, with the palm upward, to the base of the right upper arm. Immediately straighten the arms in a ripping motion, with

---

20. In the latest edition, this stance is the immovable (*fudō-dachi*). [Translator's note.]
21. It is customary to use the front (*zenkutsu*) stance. [Translator's note.]

48   **23**   49   50

clenched fists, bringing the right fist up to an upper level block and lowering the left fist in a lower level block, as shown in figure 43. At the end of the movement, the lower level blocking arm should be parallel with the forward thigh.

22. Keeping the right leg, the body, and the arms fixed in their positions, draw the left foot to the right foot.

23. Keeping the left foot in place and turning to the left, step out with the right foot to the right, i.e., away from the origin along Line 2, into a back stance.[22] At the same time, thrust the left sword hand with the palm upward forward to a point above the right knee and draw the right sword hand with the palm upward to the base of the left upper arm. Immediately straighten the arms in a ripping motion with the fists clenched to bring the left fist up to the left side in an upper level block and lower the right fist to the right in a lower level block. This movement is the mirror image of that shown in figure 43.

Yame. Without moving the left foot, slide the right foot to Line 1, in line with the left, and assume a natural stance, lowering both fists slowly, to return to the yōi stance.

BASSAI

There is a total of forty-two movements in this kata, taking about one minute to complete. The line of movement is the T type.

Yōi. As shown in figure 2, assume the feet-together (heisoku) stance and place the right fist in the left palm, the fingers of the left hand being wrapped lightly about the right fist without grasping it. The meaning of the position is protection of the testicles.

---

22. In the latest edition, this stance is the immovable (*fudō-dachi*). It is customary to use the front (*zenkutsu*) stance. [Translator's note.]

1   2   3

1. Jump out onto Line 2 with the right foot, bending the right leg upon landing, supporting the entire weight upon it, and drawing the left foot up so that it rests lightly against the back of the right foot, as shown in figure 4. During this motion, execute a middle level forearm block (uchi-uke) with the right fist, placing the left palm against the inside of the elbow as shown in the figure. The final posture is left half-facing (hanmi), with the face to the front.

2. Without moving the right foot from its position, turn the body to the left to face toward the back, assuming a front stance, the left foot being shifted back along Line 2 toward the starting point. At the same time, execute a middle level forearm block with the left fist and draw the right fist to the right hip.

3. Without altering the stance, execute a middle level block with the right fist in a motion starting from outside the left elbow, simultaneously drawing the left fist to the left hip. At the completion of the movement, the right shoulder is to be turned toward the front.

The point of these movements is to block a right fist attack from an opponent

4   1   5   6

7   **2, 3**   8   9   10

with the left fist-forearm block, followed immediately by a switching of the blocking arms and a change from a disadvantageous position (the blocker is exposed especially to a left fist or foot attack from the opponent) to an advantageous one (one relatively protected against attacks from the opponent's left side). This kind of shift is a characteristic of this kata, occurring many times in it.

4. Pivoting to the right with both feet in place, turn to face again toward the front along Line 2, at the same time executing a middle level hammer striking block (*uchikomi*) with the left fist (the arm bent at the elbow and turning with the body) and drawing the right fist to the right hip. During the motion shift to a front stance.

After the block of an attack from the rear in the preceding movement, an opponent at the front attacks and is now blocked away with the left fist while the blocker turns to face him.

5. Keeping the same stance, change fists to block with the right and retract

11   12   13   14

15   **4, 5**   16   17   18

the left fist to the hip. Note that the blocking (right) fist is to pass below and outside the elbow of the retracted (left) arm. The feeling of the motion is that of crossing the wrists of the blocking and retracted arms.

6. Shifting the full weight to the left leg without moving the left foot, move the right foot in a shallow arc through a position next to the left foot and out onto the right branch of Line 1. During this motion, while holding the right arm bent at the elbow, lower the body without breaking its upright posture, execute a lower level block to the right side in a scooping motion to the right, upward and away from the body, and then execute a right middle level hammer striking block (uchikomi) and bring the right foot to rest in a front stance. The final position of the right foot is shown in the sketch beneath figure 23.

7. Keeping the stance, switch so as to block with the left arm, and pull the right fist to the right hip. Simultaneously twist the upper trunk as much as possible to direct the left shoulder toward the front.

8. Pivoting with the feet in place, turn the body to face toward the front

19   20   21   22

23   **6, 7**   24   25   26   **8–10**

(i.e., forward along Line 2). At the same time, straighten the right leg and place the left fist, fingers toward the body, onto the right fist.

9. Without changing the stance, open the left hand, keeping the four fingers together, direct the palm downward, and extend it to the front. The intention here is to block an opponent's attack from the front with a sweeping block by the left hand from inside toward the left side.

10. Without changing the position of the body and legs, clench the left fist and draw it back to the hip, at the same time executing a middle level attack toward the front with the right fist. The meaning here is that of grasping the opponent's wrist or arm and pulling him in while attacking with the right fist.

11. Without shifting the feet, twist the body by retracting the left shoulder, simultaneously swinging the right fist as if drawing a circle toward the left to execute a middle level block as shown in figure 30, with the elbow slightly bent and the fingers upward. At the completion of the block, the right shoulder is to the front, the upper body facing to the left, and the left knee is bent. This is a

27   28   29   30   **11**

31   **12**   32   33   **13**   34

block against an attack to the chest by an opponent. Always keep the eyes on those of the opponent.

12. Without moving the feet, draw the right fist to the hip and execute a middle level attack to the front with the left fist. At the same time, straighten both legs and direct the body to the front.

Always remember that when the hand is pulled back to the hip after blocking, as in this case, one must have the feeling of grasping the opponent and pulling him in.

13. Keeping the feet in place, twist the body to the right, drawing the right shoulder back, at the same time swinging the left fist in a circle toward the right, with the elbow slightly bent and the fingers upward, to execute a middle level block. The left shoulder should be to the front, the upper body facing to the right, the right leg slightly bent, and the face to the front. This movement is the mirror image of Movement 11, shown in figure 30.

14. Keeping the left foot in place, step out along Line 2 with the right foot

35   **14**   36   **15**   37   **16**   38

39   **17**   **40**   **18**   **41**   **42**

into a left back stance, simultaneously executing a right sword hand block. The left hand is held in front of the solar plexus with the palm upward.

15. Without shifting the right foot, step forward along Line 2 with the left foot into a right back stance, at the same time executing a left sword hand block, the right hand being held in front of the solar plexus.

16. Keeping the left foot in place, move forward along Line 2 with the right foot into a left back stance, at the same time executing a right sword hand block, holding the left hand in front of the solar plexus.

17. Without moving the left foot, step back with the right foot into a right back stance, at the same time executing a left sword hand block, holding the right hand in front of the solar plexus. In other words, reverse Movement 16 to return to the final position of Movement 15.

18. Thrust the right shoulder forward, pass the right hand under the left arm, and extend it forward in a right arm block with a feeling of drawing the right leg toward the left.

19. Lift the right foot to the position shown in figure 41 and immediately thrust it forcefully downward toward the front while simultaneously clenching both fists and pulling them vigorously toward the chest, so that the left fist assumes a final position just below the right nipple.[23]

Following Movement 18, in which one has grasped the opponent's hand, one now brings the right foot up to step forcefully down onto the opponent's thigh. For this purpose, raise the right leg as high as possible while coordinating its motion with that of the arms.

20. Without changing the position of either foot, turn to the left so as to face to the rear while simultaneously executing a left middle level sword hand block, positioning the right hand in front of the solar plexus.

21. Without shifting the left foot, step forward along Line 2 (i.e., toward the point of origin) with the right foot while simultaneously executing a right

---

23. Customarily there is a kiai at this point in the kata. [Translator's note.]

43 **19** 44 45 **20** 46 **21**

47 48 49 **22** 50

middle level sword hand block and bringing the left hand in front of the solar plexus.

22. Keeping the left foot in place, draw the right foot back to the left foot while at the same time executing an upper level two-handed block, as shown in figure 49,[24] with the body facing forward. Note the position of both fists above the head, the point being to block with both wrists an opponent's two-handed upper level attack.

24. In the latest edition, this block is executed from a half-facing posture. [Translator's note.]

94   THE KATA

51   52

23. Without moving the left foot, stamp forward toward the starting point into a front stance along Line 2 with the right foot. During this motion, pull the fists vigorously apart, to a distance of about two feet, in a ripping motion over the head, then continue to swing downward, describing a semicircle with each fist, fingers inward, and finally execute middle level hammer attacks to the front from both sides with the fists, fingers upward. Motions of the hands and feet should end together. The point here is to block with both hands an opponent's two-handed attack and then to step in and attack his two sides with hammer strikes.

24. Without altering the stance, slide forward (yori-ashi) while pulling the left fist to the hip and simultaneously execute a right middle level punch. The point here is to pursue an opponent who has fallen back in surprise at the preceding attack and to deliver an immediate finishing blow.

25. Keeping the feet in place, pivot 180 degrees to the left toward the far end of Line 2, and simultaneously thrust the right sword hand forward to the

53   **23**   54   55

56   **24**   57   58   59

lower area and draw the open left hand, palm upward, to a point in front of the right shoulder. Immediately, while clenching both fists, move them apart in a ripping motion to execute with the right hand an upper level forearm block toward the front on Line 2, then draw the left foot back to the right foot. The head is to be turned to the left so that one is facing toward the front along Line 2. Refer to Movements 21 and 22 of Heian Godan.

26. Without shifting the left foot, stamp forward with the right foot along Line 2 (i.e., away from the origin) and assume a horse-riding stance, at the same time executing a right down block toward the front of Line 2, withdrawing the left fist to the hip and turning the head to face to the right.

27. Without moving the feet, face to the left and cross both arms in front of the chest, the right arm above. In a motion similar to that of drawing a bow, extend the left arm out to the left side, the hand open and the palm facing to the front, while drawing the right fist to the right hip.

28. Pivoting on the left foot, swing the right foot up in a crescent kick to

60   **25**   61   62   **26, 27**   63

64   65   66 **28–31**   67

68   69   70   71

strike the extended left palm and then lower the right foot to a position on Line 2 directly below that of the left hand at the conclusion of Movement 27,[25] at the same time executing a right elbow attack. One should be in a horse-riding stance at this point. It is important not to lower the left hand while kicking (refer to figure 29 of Heian Godan). Face toward the front, i.e., toward the space to the right of Line 2.

29. Maintaining both stance and posture, simultaneously thrust the right

---

25. It is to be noted that it is the same line as the hand, not the same point. [Translator's note.]

fist downward and clench the left fist, holding it in its position in front of the chest. The fingers of both fists are turned toward the body. The point here is a lower level block with the right fist and protection of the solar plexus region with the left fist.

30. In the same stance and posture, thrust the left fist downward and bring the right fist up in front of the chest. The lowered arm should pass on the inside in this motion.

31. Keeping the same stance and posture, simultaneously thrust the right fist downward and bring the left fist up in front of the chest. The final position here is identical to that of Movement 29.

32. Keeping both feet in place and assuming a front stance, withdraw the left fist, with palm upward, to the left hip and place the right fist on the left fist with palm turned inward. Face to the right (i.e., toward the origin of Line 2).

33. Keeping the same stance, attack to the front simultaneously with both fists, the left in an upper level attack, fingers downward, the right in a lower level attack, fingers upward. The fists should define a vertical line. This position is shown in figure 76.

34. Without moving the left foot, draw the right foot back to the left, simultaneously pulling the right fist back to the right hip and placing the left fist on it with the right palm turned upward, the left toward the body.

35. Without moving the right foot, execute a stamping step[26] with the left foot toward the rear along Line 2 into a left front stance, simultaneously executing an upper level attack with the right fist, fingers downward and a lower level attack with the left fist, fingers upward. This is the mirror image of the position shown in figure 76.

36. Without moving the right foot, pull the left foot back to the right foot while placing the two fists at the left hip.

---

26. In the latest edition, the stamping steps in Movements 35–37 are front kicks. [Translator's note.]

98   THE KATA

76   77   78   **34**   79

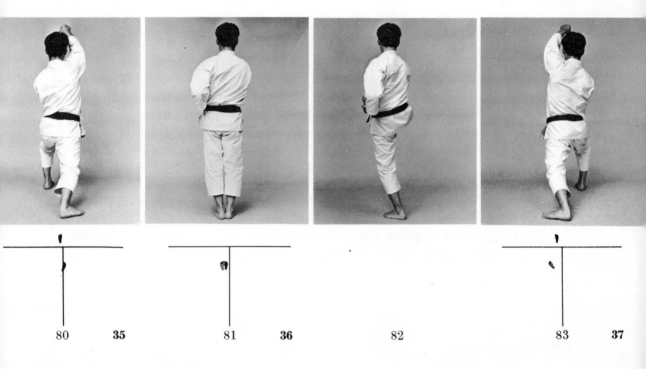

80   **35**   81   **36**   82   83   **37**

37. Keeping the left foot in place, perform a right stomping step toward the rear along Line 2, simultaneously executing an upper level attack with the left fist, fingers downward, and a lower level attack with the right fist, fingers upward.[27] This is the same as Movement 33.

Movements 33 to 37 are a three-time repetition (right-left-right) of a movement. Such units occur frequently in the various kata, in this case the repeated technique being that employed when one's hair is grasped by an opponent;

27. Customarily there is a kiai at this point in the kata. [Translator's note.]

84   85   86

while looking steadily at the opponent and without trying to move the head from the position to which it is pulled, attack simultaneously to the philtrum and lower abdomen with the two fists. This is an example of the tactic, "Cut his meat while cutting your skin" (i.e., take a cut skin to inflict a cut muscle).

38. Pivoting on the right foot, swing the left leg counterclockwise to align the feet in a wide stance along Line 1; then bring the right fist down from shoulder level to the left side as if drawing a circle and execute a lower level forearm block. At the same time, withdraw the left fist to the hip and draw the left shoulder back so that the right shoulder extends to the front. The left leg assumes a front stance naturally.

39. Without shifting either foot, while pulling the right fist back to the hip and drawing the right shoulder back, swing the left fist from the shoulder level down and to the right in a large circle and perform a left lower level forearm block. At this point, the left shoulder should be toward the front and the body in a half-facing posture, as in Movement 38. The right leg goes naturally into

87   **38**   88   89   90

91   92   **39**   93   94

95   96   **40**   97

a front stance. This technique is employed to scoop and immediately throw back an opponent's foot, so it is essential to sweep as low as possible.

40. Pull the left foot half the distance in toward the right; then step out along Line 2 with the right foot into a left back stance, at the same time executing a right sword hand block and positioning the left hand in front of the solar plexus and facing to the front.

41. Without moving the left foot, while turning the face half left, move the body back onto Line 1, maintaining the right hand and foot in the sword hand position.

98　　**41**　　　　99　　　　　100　　　　101

102　　　　　103

42. Without turning the head, draw the right foot close to the left foot, then advance diagonally to the front with the left foot into a right back stance, at the same time executing a left sword hand block and positioning the right hand in front of the chest. For the sword hand posture, refer to Heian Shodan.

Yame. At the command "Yame," hold the right foot in place and draw the left foot to the right foot, returning the hands to the yōi position.

| 1 | 2 | **1, 2** | 3 | 4 |

KWANKŪ

This kata consists of sixty-five movements and requires about two minutes to complete.[28] The line of movement is of the plus-minus type.

Yōi. With feet apart in a natural stance and the arms straight, place the hands in front of the groin. With the hands opened, fingers together, and thumbs extended, place the right thumb and fingertips on those of the left. The palms of both hands are directed toward the body. This position of the hands closely resembles that of the Ogasawara school of etiquette. Refer to figure 2.

1. Maintaining the position of the hands relative to each other, raise them slowly and position them at a point above the head as shown in figure 3. Sight through the opening formed by the hands.

2. With a feeling of violently rending the formed position of the hands, draw them apart to a distance of about one foot,[29] then slowly lower them to either side as if describing a circle, bringing the left hand to a position in front of the groin, the palm facing to the right front, and the right hand so that the edge is placed along the left palm, the two palms perpendicular, the right palm facing diagonally to the left front.

Note that the preceding movements have the double meaning of demonstrating that one is unarmed and of protecting one's groin. This sort of double meaning is essentially that implied by the description "Two is one, one is two," applied to the yin-yang symbol.

3. Moving the left foot a step to the left into a right back stance, as shown in

---

28. This kata is *Kankū* in Japanese. This edition retains the Okinawan Kwankū. [Translator's note.]

29. It must be realized that Master Funakoshi was a short man by modern standards; a taller man would have to adjust the hand separation to execute the movement properly. [Translator's note.]

5   6   7   **3**   8

figure 7, execute an upper level block with the open left hand, palm directed to the right. Place the right spear hand in front of the chest holding the hand at a slightly higher level than for a sword hand block. Face to the left.

4. Pivoting with the feet in place, shift to a left back stance while executing an upper level block with the open right hand and bringing the left spear hand in front of the chest. This is the mirror image of the position shown in figure 7. The face is turned to the right.

5. Pivoting with the feet in place, face to the front, straightening the knees, and bring the right hand from its position to the right and rear forward and then back in a circular motion to end with the fist at the right hip, while at the same time placing the left hand, with palm downward, under the right upper arm and drawing it toward the front along the lower surface of the right arm until it is extended horizontally to the front. Refer to figure 12. The point of this motion of the right hand is to draw an opponent's arm inward, that of the left hand to block from the inside an attack from the opponent.

9   **4**   10   11   12   **5, 6**

13   14   15   7   16   8

6. Clenching the left fist and drawing it to the left hip, execute a middle level attack with the right fist. It is important that one maintain an upright posture and especially that he not extend the right shoulder too far to the front.

7. Keeping the feet in place, swing the right fist in a circular motion to execute a middle level forearm block, extending the right shoulder to the front and drawing the left shoulder toward the back and the left fist to the left hip. That is, rotate the trunk to the left to assume a half-facing posture. The left leg will bend naturally. Refer to figure 30 of Bassai.

8. Without moving the feet, rotate the trunk again to the front and execute a middle level attack with the left fist, drawing the right fist to the hip. At this time straighten both knees.

9. Without moving the feet, twist the upper body to the right and at the same time execute a middle level forearm block with the left arm. The left shoulder is extended to the front, the right shoulder is pulled to the rear, and the right fist remains at the right hip. Note that Movements 7, 8 and 9 are the same as Movements 11, 12 and 13 in Bassai.

17   18   9   19   20   10, 11

21   22   **12**   23   **13**   24   **14**

10. Draw the left foot halfway in from the left, look to the back, place the two fists at the left hip, the right on the left with the fingers of the left fist upward, those of the right toward the body, and bring the sole of the right foot against the inside of the left leg just above the knee. This position is similar to that shown in figure 8 of Heian Nidan.

11. Execute an upper level attack to an opponent at the back with the right back fist, while at the same time striking out with the right sword foot to the opponent's testicles. This movement is similar to Movement 8 of Heian Nidan.

12. While lowering the right foot into a right back stance and looking along Line 2 toward the front, execute a left middle level sword hand block, placing the right spear hand in front of the solar plexus. This is the same as in Heian Nidan; as indicated there, one is to execute this movement and the preceding one in rapid, continuous succession.

13. Without shifting the left foot, step forward with the right foot onto Line 2 into a left back stance, at the same time executing a right middle level sword hand block.

14. Keeping the right foot in place, step forward with the left along Line 2 into a right back stance, executing a left middle level sword hand block.

15. Without shifting the left foot, while stepping forward with the right foot, execute a middle level attack with the right spear hand, palm facing to the left, sliding the left hand, palm downward, along the lower surface of the right arm up to the armpit.[30] Note that Movements 10 to 15 are identical to the sequence cited in Heian Nidan, and one should refer to explanations for that sequence.

16. Keeping the feet in place, turn counterclockwise to face to the rear along Line 2, swing the right hand in a large arc that brings the back of the hand almost in contact with the forehead and then forward in a right sword hand attack with the palm turning upward at the moment of focus. At the same time, execute an upper level block with the open left hand, with the back of the hand

---

30. Customarily, the front stance is used in this movement, and there is a kiai at this point in the kata. [Translator's note.]

25   26   **15**   27   28

facing the forehead. The main point of the sixteenth and seventeenth movements is the same as those of the eleventh and twelfth movements of Heian
Yodan.

17. Kick toward the tip of the extended right hand with the right foot.

18. Lowering the right foot to Line 2 and pivoting through 180 degrees to
face forward along Line 2, at the same time thrust the right sword hand toward
the front lower level, parallel to the upper surface of the left thigh, and place
the left sword hand in front of the right shoulder, both palms directed upward.
Then, clenching the fists and drawing them apart in a ripping motion, bring the
right fist back in an upper level forearm block, the palm toward the head,
toward the rear along Line 2 while extending the left fist toward the front along
Line 2 in a down block. During this motion, assume a right back stance, continuing to look forward along Line 2.

19. Keeping both feet in place, again thrust the right sword hand to the lower
level in front and place the left sword hand in front of the right shoulder, both
palms upward.

29   **16**   30   **17**   31   32

| 33 | **18, 19** | 34 | 35 | **20** | 36 |

20. Keeping the right foot in place and straightening the knees, draw the left foot slightly in toward the right. At the same time, clench the fists and draw them apart, bringing the right fist to the right hip and swinging the left arm horizontally out to the left (i.e., toward the front along Line 2), with palm downward. Face along the left arm.

21. Rotating the trunk to face toward the front along Line 2 without moving the feet, swing the right sword hand in a wide arc carrying it past the forehead toward the front, with palm upward, moving the left sword hand in an upper level block so that it is brought in front of the forehead, with the palm forward, at the moment of focus of the right sword hand.

22. Kick to the front with the right foot, touching the tip of the right hand.

23. Lowering the right foot to the front along Line 2 in a movement similar to that in Movement 18, pivot counterclockwise to the rear and thrust the right sword hand toward the lower level, placing the left sword hand in front of the right shoulder. Immediately clench the fists and draw them apart, the right to

| 37 | 38 | 39 | **21** | 40 | **22** |

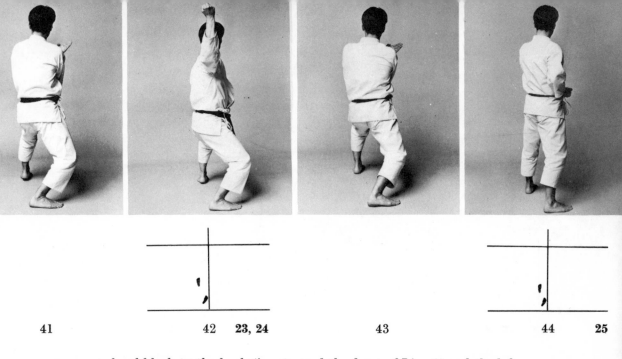

41   42   **23, 24**   43   44   **25**

an upper level block to the back (i.e., toward the front of Line 2) and the left fist to a down block toward the front. During this movement, assume a right back stance and turn the face to the left, i.e., toward the rear of Line 2.

24. Keeping both feet in place, again thrust the right sword hand toward the lower level and position the left sword hand at the right shoulder.

25. Without moving the right foot, straighten up and, drawing the left foot slightly in toward the right, clench both fists and draw them past each other, the right fist to the right hip and the left horizontally out to the left side toward the rear of Line 2. This is the same as Movement 20.

26. Placing both fists at the right hip, the left on the right, with the palm of the right upward, that of the left toward the body, face to the left (i.e., along the right branch of Line 3) and place the left foot above the knee on the inside of the right leg in the initial position for a left side kick.

27. Execute simultaneously a left upper level back fist attack and a left side kick with the left sword foot toward the right branch of Line 3.

45   **26, 27**   46   47   **28**

48 **29, 30**   49   50   51

28. Lowering the left foot onto the right branch of Line 3 in a left front stance, strike the right elbow with the left palm. Movements 27 to 31 are the same as those in which the side kick is executed in Heian Yodan, and one should refer to the description given there.

29. Straighten up, bring the right foot to the left foot, face to the right (i.e., along the left branch of Line 3), placing both fists at the left hip, then slide the sole of the right foot up the left leg to a point above the knee.

30. Simultaneously execute a right upper level back fist attack and a right side kick, using the right sword foot, to the right (i.e., along the left branch of Line 3).

31. Lowering the kicking foot to the left branch of Line 3 into a front stance, attack to the right with the left elbow, striking the elbow with the right palm. While lowering the right foot, there should be a suggestion of drawing the left foot in slightly. This same point applies in Movement 28.

32. Keeping both feet in place and assuming a right back stance, face to the left along the right branch of Line 3 and execute a left sword hand block.

33. Without moving the left foot, step diagonally to the front with the right foot into a left back stance and execute a right sword hand block. Reference should be made to Movements 13 to 16 of Heian Nidan, which are identical to Movements 32 to 35.

34. Pivoting with the left foot in place, return the right foot to Line 3 in a left back stance and execute a right sword hand block.

35. Pivoting on the right foot, step diagonally to the front with the left foot, assuming a right back stance, and execute a left sword hand block.

36. Without moving the right foot and bringing the left toward the rear along Line 2, attack with the right sword hand in a motion bringing it almost in contact with the forehead and then swinging to the right and horizontally outward toward the front (i.e., toward the rear of Line 2), the palm facing upward. The left sword hand is brought upward in an upper level block, coming in

110   THE KATA

52 **31**	53	54 **32**	55 **33**

front of the forehead with the palm to the front at the moment of focus of the right hand. During this motion, one should assume a front stance with the right shoulder directed to the front, the trunk rotated to the left. This movement is the same as Movements 16 and 21.

37. Kick the tip of the right hand with the right foot and immediately retract the kicking foot.

38. Jump forward toward the rear of Line 2, landing on the right foot with the right leg bent and supporting the full body weight and the left foot drawn up just behind and lightly touching the right, at the same time extending the left hand to the front as if grasping an object, then pulling it back to the left hip, and swinging the right hand in a large arc that brings it almost in contact with the stomach and chest and then outward in an upper level back fist attack to the front. The motions of the hands and feet must end simultaneously. Reference should be made to the description of the jump-in technique of Heian Yodan, which is the same as the present one.

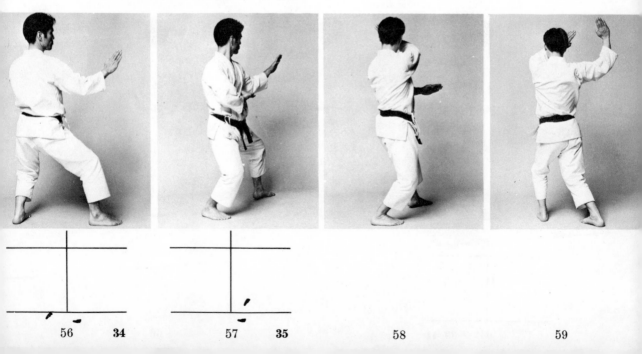

56 **34**	57 **35**	58	59

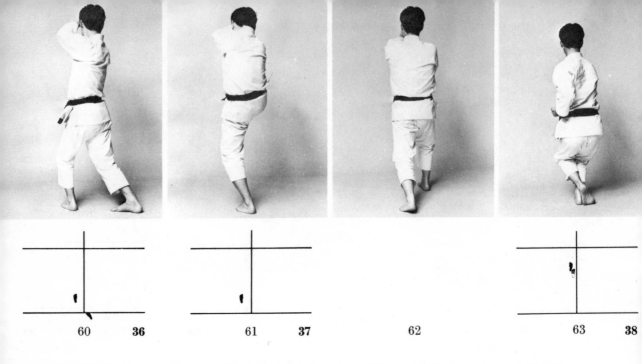

60 **36** 61 **37** 62 63 **38**

39. Step backward with the left foot to assume a front stance, at the same time executing a middle level forearm block with the right fist.

40. Without altering the position of the hips and legs, draw the right fist to the hip and execute a middle level reverse punch with the left fist.

41. Keeping the hips and legs fixed, pull the left fist back to the hip and execute a middle level attack with the right fist. Movements 40 and 41 are a continuous attack (renzuki) technique and are to be executed in rapid succession.

42. Pivoting counterclockwise on the left foot to face to the rear (i.e., toward the front of Line 2), draw the right knee up high to the body and, with the palms sliding forward along the sides of the raised thigh, thrust forward to the midsection with the right fist, fingers upward, and place the left hand on the inner surface of the right wrist.

43. Without moving the left foot, lower the right foot to the front into a

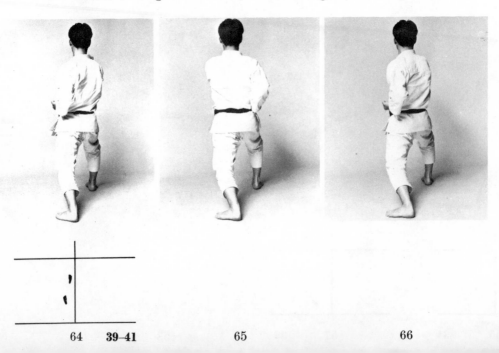

64 **39–41** 65 66

67   **42**   68   69   **43**   70

71   72   73   **44**   74   **45**

front stance and rest the fingertips[31] of both hands on the floor as shown in figure 69. It is important to look to the front during this movement.

This is a stance peculiar to Kwankū, used in a stalemate situation in which each opponent has apparently exhausted his potential. The one now suddenly drops his body to the ground to startle the opponent for an attack.

44. Pivoting with the feet in place, twist the upper body counterclockwise to face toward the rear in a right back stance and execute a lower level block to

31. In the latest edition, the palms are down on the floor (figure 71 and 72). [Translator's note.]

75   76   **46, 47**   77   78   **48–50**

the left with the left sword hand. The left palm is parallel to and about six to seven inches above the left thigh. The right sword hand is placed below the left nipple with the palm upward.

45. Keeping the left foot in place, step forward (i.e., toward the rear of Line 2) with the right foot, assuming a left back stance, and execute a right sword hand block.

46. Pivoting counterclockwise on the right foot, step with the left foot onto the left branch of Line 1 into a front stance while executing a middle level forearm block to the left with the left fist and pulling the right fist to the right hip.

47. Without moving the feet, draw the left fist back and execute a right middle level reverse punch.

48. Pivoting with the feet in place, turn the body to the right to assume a front stance and execute a right forearm block with the right fist, drawing the left fist to the hip.

49. Maintaining the posture of the body, execute a left middle level reverse punch, drawing the right fist back to the hip.

50. Maintaining the posture of the body, draw the left fist back to the hip and execute a middle level attack with the right fist. Movements 49 and 50 constitute a continuous attack (renzuki).

51. Turning to the right with the weight on the left foot, come to face to the rear of Line 2 while drawing the right foot up to the side of the left knee and placing both fists at the left hip, the one on top of the other, to assume the initial stance of the right side kick.

52. Standing on the left leg, execute an upper level attack to the rear of Line 2 with the right back fist while kicking to the lower level with the right sword foot.

53. Simultaneously lower the right foot to the rear of Line 2 to assume a right back stance, facing toward the front of Line 2, and execute a left middle level sword hand block.

114 THE KATA

79   80   81   **51, 52**   82

54. Advancing a step along Line 2 with the right foot, execute a middle level attack with the right spear hand, palm to the left, while sliding the left sword hand, palm downward, along the lower surface of the right arm to bring it up to the armpit.

55. As if responding to one's right arm being twisted to the right (the opposite of the analogous situation in Heian Sandan), pivot to the left on the right foot to advance a step along Line 2, assuming a horse-riding stance. During the turn, bring the right forearm in a twisting motion to a position over the right shoulder while executing an upper level attack to the left (i.e., toward the front of Line 2) in a wide motion with the left back fist. The right fist should be drawn back to the right hip so that its motion is completed at the instant of focus of the left back fist attack. Face along the left arm.

56. Maintaining the posture of the body, shift sideways (yori-ashi) to the left (i.e., forward along Line 2), with both feet and execute a left upper level back fist attack in a large circular motion of the fist.

83   **53**   84   85   **54**

86   87   88   89

90 55   91   92 56   93 57

57. Keeping the feet in place, rotate the trunk and attack with the right elbow to the left along Line 2, striking the right elbow with the left palm. During the motion the left foot adjusts naturally so that one assumes a front stance.

58. Pivoting with the feet in place to face toward the rear of Line 2, shift to a front stance, the trunk directed toward the right branch of Line 3, and place one fist over the other at the left hip.

59. Without changing the stance, execute a down block with the right fist.

60. As shown in figure 96, pivot on the right foot to step toward the rear of

116 THE KATA

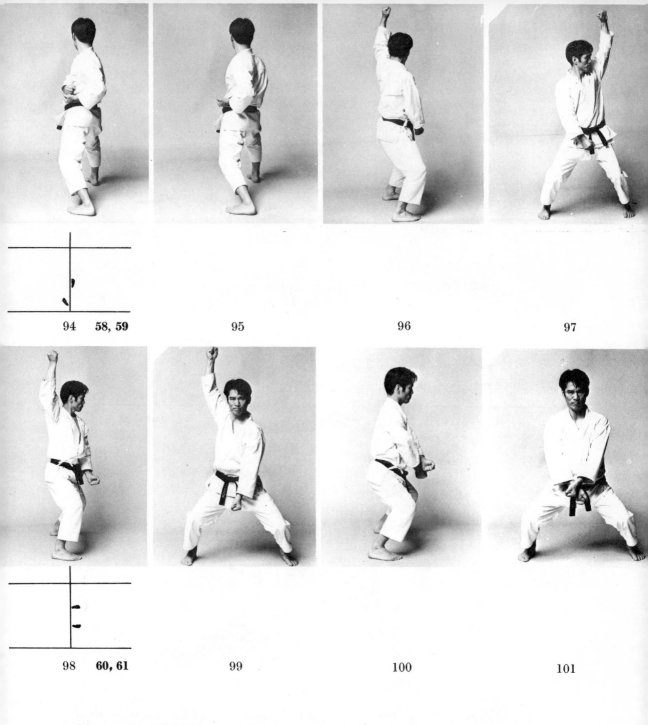

94   **58, 59**   95   96   97

98   **60, 61**   99   100   101

Line 2 with the left foot, moving into a horse-riding stance. At the same time, strike downward from over the head in a wide motion of the left fist and swing the right fist upward.

61. Without changing the stance, attack downward, the right fist passing inside the left to form a cross with the fists as shown in figure 101.

62. Standing in the same position, open the fists and thrust the hands up over the head with the wrists still crossed, at the same time straightening the legs.

63. With the wrists still crossed over the head, pivot to the right on the right

102   **62**   103   104   **63, 64**

105   106

foot as shown in figure 104, bringing the left foot onto the forward segment of Line 2 and assuming a front stance facing toward the rear of Line 2.

64. Maintaining the posture of the body, clench the fists, keeping the wrists crossed, and lower them to just below eye level.

65. Facing toward the rear of Line 2, kick high with the left foot and follow immediately with a high right kick, the latter being executed before the left foot touches the ground.[32] At the same time, move the left hand as if grasping

---

32. Customarily there is a kiai at this point in the kata at the start of the jump. [Translator's note].

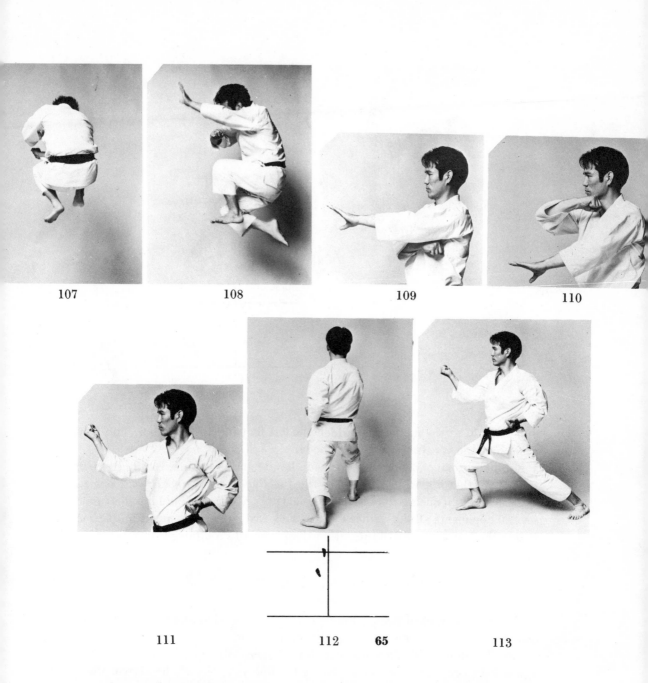

107   108   109   110

111   112   **65**   113

something in front and then back to the left hip, and with the right hand execute an upper level back fist attack to the front (i.e., toward the rear of Line 2), in a wide circular motion bringing the fist from the lower abdomen across the chest to the front. The feet should land on the floor to form a front stance at the instant of completion of the hand motions.

Yame. Pivoting to the right on the right foot and stepping out onto the left branch of Line 1 with the left foot, bend the trunk forward and swing the right fist, with palm upward, from the inside outward toward the right in a circular downward block, both fists coming finally into a natural position in front of the

114   115

upper thighs at the moment at which the left foot touches the floor. The final position is the yōi stance of Heian Shodan.

Kwankū is one of the longest forms in karate and is so varied in its scope of techniques that it is widely known as the *Fighting Form against Eight Enemies*. Many feel that if one masters this form, he will be able to defend himself against several opponents at once, since even in such cases attacks come at most from two or three at any one instant, rather than from all simultaneously.

TEKKI SHODAN

This kata consists of twenty-nine movements and takes about one minute to complete. The line of movement is the straight line.

Yōi. Standing in the feet-together stance, open both hands and hold them in a position to guard the testicles, placing the fingers of the left hand over those of the right. The open hands imply as well the second meaning that one has no weapons. Consistent with the first meaning of protection of the testicles, the hands should be held slightly away from the body.

1. Turning the head to face to the right, as shown in figure 3, pass the left foot lightly over the right and, without moving the right foot or altering the posture, cross the legs to place the left foot to the right of the right foot on the line of movement. In this movement, there is a feeling of lowering the hips. The movement is preparatory to a defense against an opponent from the right.

2. Without moving the left foot, continue to look to the right and take a

large step to the right with the right foot into a horse-riding stance, at the same time placing the left fist at the hip and extending the right arm out to the right side, palm to the front, in a circular motion past the front of the right shoulder. During the motion, assume the posture shown in figure 4.

The basic stance of the Tekki forms is explained in some detail in the section on stances in chapter 2, and reference and careful study of the discussion there should be made. This standing form is the essential point of this form and must be practiced with particular care. The meaning of the present movement is that of hooking and blocking an attack from the right side with the right wrist.

3. Keeping the body fixed from the waist down, rotate the trunk to the right as shown in figure 5 and execute a left elbow attack, at the same time striking the palm of the right hand against the left elbow with a sense of drawing an opponent into the elbow. In applying the elbow attack, one keeps the fist clenched, fingers toward the body, and holds the forearm parallel to the plane of the chest and about six to seven inches from it. It is essential in this move-

ment that only the upper part of the body be rotated, the lower part being held in its original posture.

4. Keeping the lower part of the body fixed, face to the left along Line 1 and simultaneously place the right fist at the hip and the left fist, palm inward, onto the right, as shown in figure 6. Note that the trunk is turned directly to the front, with care given not to raise the shoulders, and only the face is directed to the left.

5. Without altering the stance, execute a lower level block with the left fist, bringing it first to a point in front of the right shoulder. This is the position shown in figure 7. The left fist is positioned about six to seven inches above the left thigh, the motion being identical to the first block of Heian Shodan in every respect except for the change in stance to horse riding.

6. Without altering the stance, simultaneously draw the left fist to the left hip in a rotating motion and position the right fist in front of the chest as shown in figure 8.

In this position of the right arm, which is intended as a protection of the solar plexus, the forearm is parallel to the plane of the chest at the level of the solar plexus and about six to seven inches from the chest. The fist, which is not to extend beyond the left side of the body, is placed slightly lower than the elbow, making a slight decline in the forearm from the elbow to the fist (the *mizu-nagare* or "water-flowing" position).

7. Keeping the left foot in place, pass the right foot lightly over the left, as shown in figure 9, without altering the posture of the rest of the body. Note that this movement, which is preparatory to defense against an opponent to the left, is to be made with the hips low.

8. Keeping the right foot in place, take a large step to the left with the left foot into a horse-riding stance, simultaneously turning the face to the front and rotating the right forearm up in a middle level forearm block to assume the position shown in figure 11. The right fist should be slightly below eye level, and the point of the elbow about six to seven inches from the body.

122 THE KATA

13   14   15   16   13

9. Without altering the stance, pass the right fist across in front of the left shoulder, with the fingers upward, and bring the left fist to the front of the body into the transitional position shown in figure 12.

10. As shown in figure 13, continue immediately to extend the right arm downward to the front and right side in a lower level block, the back of the fist directed forward, and simultaneously execute a middle level block with the left arm, the fist stopping above the left shoulder, fingers toward the head.[33] This movement should be executed forcefully, the right fist sliding through the crook of the left elbow and downward and the left fist swinging upward. The point of this movement is a defense against simultaneous attack with a fist and a foot.

11. Follow immediately with a left back fist attack to the front, placing the right wrist, fingers downward, below the left elbow as shown in figure 14.

Movements 9 to 11 are techniques identified with the horse-riding stance and require diligent practice because of their considerable difficulty. Although they have been treated separately to facilitate description, they are in fact to be executed in a single motion. The point of Movement 11 is to draw an opponent's attacking fist downward and toward the body with the right hand and to counterattack to the upper jaw with the left back fist. Hence, the left fist must end in a position directly in front of the face.

12. Without altering the stance of the preceding movement, face to the left as shown in figure 15.

13. Without altering the posture of the trunk, kick the left foot upward and inward as shown in figure 16. The sole of the left foot should reach a level above that of the right knee. The purpose of this movement is to ward off a kicking attack from an opponent. After learning them well, one should execute Movements 13 and 14 as a single, continuous motion.

---

33. After completing the middle level block, the left arm continues without perceptible pause from in front of the body up to the position above the left shoulder. [Translator's note.]

17   14, 15   18   19   16   20   17-24

14. Thrust the left foot down forcefully into its previous position (horse-riding stance), at the same time rotating the left fist clockwise until the palm is directed downward and twisting the body to the left as shown in figure 17. Throughout the motion, the right fist is maintained in its position at the point of the left elbow. One must give particular care not to alter the position of the hips and legs in turning the trunk to the left. The point to this technique is to thrust the foot down onto an opponent's leg while blocking his fist attack with the left wrist.

15. Without altering the stance, turn only the head to face to the right as shown in figure 18. The purpose of this movement is to prepare for an attack sensed from the right.

16. Without altering the posture of the body above the waist, kick the right foot upward as shown in figure 19. The sole of the right foot should come higher than the level of the left knee. Note that the left leg remains bent, and the hips in their low position. The entire movement is the mirror image of Movement 13. After learning this movement well, it is to be executed continuously with Movement 17.

17. Drive the right foot forcefully back to its original position (horse-riding stance), at the same time rotating the trunk to the right to execute a middle level block with the left arm, fingers upward, as shown in figure 20. The purpose of this movement, together with the preceding one, is to sweep an opponent's kick with the right foot and to follow immediately by simultaneously attacking his supporting leg and blocking his middle level attack.

18. Without altering the stance below the waist, face to the left as shown in figure 21, the trunk directed squarely to the front, and simultaneously draw the right fist back to the hip and place the left fist, fingers to the back, on the right. This motion, with the turning of the head to the left, is preparatory to receiving an opponent from the left sensed while one is engaged in blocking an attack from the right.

19. Maintaining the stance, thrust both fists to the left from their on-guard

124 THE KATA

position at the right hip, the left arm to extend straight out to the left and, as shown in figure 22, the right to be bent at the elbow so that the forearm is about six to seven inches from the chest and the fist below the level of the shoulder and about even with the left side of the body.[34]

This is a type of double-hand attack (morote-zuki). The left fist blocks to the outside an attack from the left and attacks the middle level of the opponent while the right fist either guards the chest or itself attacks. In actual practice, the body could be rotated more to the left with the right fist attacking the opponent's chest.

20. Without altering the stance, draw the right fist to the right hip, open the left fist, and block an attack from the left in a hooking motion with the left wrist, palm to the front, as shown in figure 24. The final position is the mirror image of that of Movement 2.

21. Without altering the stance below the waist, rotate the trunk to the left and attack with the right elbow as shown in figure 25, the right fist remaining clenched with the fingers inward. At the same time, strike the elbow with the left hand in a motion indicating the grasping and pulling forward of an opponent. This is the mirror image of Movement 3. One must take care not to break the stance of the hips and legs.

22. Without altering the stance of the hips and legs, face to the right, the trunk directed to the front, and draw the left fist to the left hip, placing the right fist, fingers inward, on the left as shown in figure 26. This is the mirror image of Movement 4.

23. Without altering the stance, move the right fist through a point in front of the left shoulder and downward into a lower level block to the right side, the final position being that shown in figure 27. This is the mirror image of Movement 5.

24. Without altering the stance, retract the right fist to the hip in a forceful

---

34. Customarily there is a kiai at this point in the kata. [Translator's note.]

25   26   27   28

twisting motion and position the left fist in front of the chest with the forearm in a horizontal plane as shown in figure 28. The front of the left fist should not extend beyond the side of the body. The forearm should be about six to seven inches from the chest with the slight water-flowing (mizu-nagare) decline in the line from the elbow to the fist.

25. Without altering the posture of the body above the waist, and holding the right foot in place, pass the left foot lightly over the right toward the right side, as shown in figure 29. During this motion, it is important to hold the hips low and bend the knees. The hips should move at a constant level whether the legs are crossing or assuming an open stance.

26. Keeping the left foot in place, take a large step to the right with the right foot into a horse-riding stance, at the same time executing a middle level forearm block with the left fist while facing directly to the front, as shown in figure 31. This is the mirror image of Movement 8.

27. Without altering the stance, bring the left fist up in front of the right

29   25   30   31   26-30   32

126 THE KATA

shoulder, fingers inward, as shown in figure 32 and extend the right fist downward and to the front, fingers downward.

28. Without pausing, draw the fists apart in a ripping motion, the right fist upward to the right as shown in figure 33, fingers toward the head, and the left fist downward, fingers downward. The meaning of the movement is a block with both wrists against an opponent's simultaneous fist and foot attacks.

29. Without pausing, rotate the back of the right fist toward the back, drawing the fist back above the right shoulder, then swing it downward to the front, at the same time positioning the left wrist under the point of the right elbow as shown in figure 34.

Like Movements 9 to 11, Movements 27 to 29 are to be executed quickly in a single, continuous motion. The point of the motion of the right fist in the present movement is to attack an opponent's philtrum with the knuckles of the fist; one should face directly to the front.

30. Without altering the stance, face to the right as shown in figure 35.

31. Without altering the posture, kick upward to the inside with the right foot as shown in figure 36. The sole of the right foot should be brought up to a level above that of the left knee, while the hips are to be maintained in a low position and the left leg bent. After learning the movements well, this and the next movement are to be executed as a single motion.

32. Thrusting the right foot forcefully down into its previous position, rotate the body and arms toward the right as shown in figure 37 and execute a middle level block. During the block, rotate the right wrist completely, so that the back of the fist comes to be directed upward, while continuing to hold the left fist at the point of the right elbow.

33. Without altering the stance, face toward the left as shown in figure 38.

34. Without altering the posture, kick up quickly toward the center with the left foot as shown in figure 39. The sole of the left foot should be brought up to a level above that of the right knee. The hips are to be kept in a low position

TEKKI SHODAN 127

37 **32, 33**   38   39 **34**   40 **35–37**

41   42   43   44

and the right leg bent. Having learned these techniques well, one should execute this and the following movement in a single motion.

35. Thrusting the left foot forcefully back into its previous position, rotate the trunk and arms toward the left as shown in figure 40 and execute a middle level block. The hips and legs are to be fixed firmly in the horse-riding stance.

36. Without altering the stance of the hips and legs, face to the right, turning the body squarely to the front, draw the left fist back to the hip, and place the right fist on the left as shown in figure 41.

37. Without altering the stance, thrust both fists simultaneously out to the right as shown in figure 42.[35] Note that the right arm is fully extended to the

---

35. Customarily there is a kiai at this point in the kata. [Translator's note.]

right side, while the left elbow is bent so that the forearm is positioned six to seven inches in front of the chest and the left fist in line with the right side of the body.

Yame. At the command of "Yame," holding the left foot in place, draw the right foot toward the left, returning the hands and feet slowly to the yōi position, then turn the head slowly to face to the front.

Although this kata has been divided into thirty-seven movements to facilitate description, certain groups, i.e., nine to eleven, thirteen and fourteen, sixteen and seventeen, twenty-seven to twenty-nine, thirty-one and thirty-two, thirty-four and thirty-five, are properly considered to be single movements, so that it consists in fact of twenty-nine movements.

TEKKI NIDAN

There are twenty-six movements in this form, taking about one minute to perform. The line of movement is the straight line, as in Tekki Shodan.

Yōi. Stand at the left end of the line of movement in the natural stance, the heels apart and the fists held naturally in front of the upper thighs. This is identical to the yōi stance of Heian Shodan.

1. As shown in figure 2, while turning the head to face to the right and without moving the right foot, step lightly with the left foot over the right to cross the legs and bend the arms at the elbows, bringing the forearms up into a horizontal position with the fists just below the level of the nipples. This stance, with the chest protected, is one of readiness against an opponent on the right.

2. Holding the left foot in place and taking a big step to the right with the right foot into a horse-riding stance, first move the forearms upward to bring both fists, with the fingers downward, to the level of the chin. Then, using this initial momentum, continue this motion smoothly into a middle level block with the right fist, fingers downward, as shown in figure 4, the left

1   2   1   3   4   2

TEKKI NIDAN 129

5 3 6 4 7 5 8

forearm positioned horizontally in front of the chest, fingers downward. Note that one should be facing toward the right at the end of the movement, with the right fist at the level of the shoulder and the point of the right elbow six to seven inches from the side of the body. The point of the movement is an inside block with the right wrist of an attack from the right and protection of the chest with the left fist.

3. Keeping the right foot in place and crossing the left foot lightly over it while continuing to face to the right, straighten the right arm out toward the front by swinging it inward from the right, fingers upward. At the same time, place the opened left hand lightly at the inside of the right elbow. The left hand is just below chest level. The right arm is held straight and the left forearm is parallel to the plane of the chest. The meaning of the movement is to block an attack sensed to come from the front while continuing to face to the right on guard against the opponent from that direction.

4. Without moving the left foot, take a big step to the right with the right foot into a horse-riding stance. At the same time, while maintaining the posture of the trunk and head, swing the right fist out to the right, fingers upward, holding the left hand still in place at the right elbow. The right fist should come to rest slightly above hip level. The movement deflects a middle level attack from the right with a block using the right wrist.

5. Keeping the right foot in place, draw the left foot to the right and straighten the knees to assume the feet-together stance. At the same time, face to the left and bring the fists, fingers downward, to chest level, as shown in figure 7, the elbows extending out to either side.

6. Continuing to face to the left and keeping the right foot in place, take a big step to the left with the left foot into a horse-riding stance and block to the left, starting the arm movement by raising both forearms, the backs of the fists turning outward to the sides, to obtain momentum and then continuing smoothly into a middle level block with the left fist, fingers downward, placing the right forearm in a horizontal position in front of the chest, fingers down-

130 THE KATA

<table>
<tr><td>9</td><td>6</td><td>10</td><td>7</td><td>11</td><td>8–10</td><td>12</td></tr>
</table>

ward. The final position is the mirror image of that shown in figure 4. The movement is the mirror image of Movement 2.

7. Continuing to face to the left with the body directed to the front, cross the right foot lightly over the left. At the same time, swing the left fist toward the center, fingers upward, so that the left arm extends toward the front with the opened right hand placed on the inner margin of the left elbow. This is the mirror image of Movement 3. The left fist should be at the level of the solar plexus, causing the right elbow to be somewhat elevated, and the right forearm parallel to the plane of the chest.

8. Take a big step to the left with the left foot into a horse-riding stance without altering the body posture or shifting the right foot. Simultaneously swing the left fist, fingers upward, out to the left, the right hand being held in place at the left elbow. This movement is the mirror image of Movement 4. Note that the fist is at approximately hip level, the left elbow straightened.

9. Without altering the stance of the hips or legs, turn the face to the right, bring the right fist to the left hip, the back of the fist directed to the front, and having opened the left fist, place the palm of the left hand against the right fist, the back of the left hand directed to the left side.

10. Without altering the stance of the hips and legs and continuing to face to the right, execute a right middle level block with the right fist, fingers upward, holding the left hand throughout the motion on the inner margin of the right forearm with the fingertips at the right wrist as shown in figure 13. Contact of the left hand and right arm should not be broken during the motion. The body continues to be directed toward the front.

11. Keeping the left foot in place, look to the front and raise the right knee up high. At the same time, draw the right fist back to the right hip in a smooth motion, fingers upward, and place the palm of the left hand against the right fist as shown in figure 14, with the back of the hand directed to the front.

12. Stamp the right foot down strongly into its former position to assume a horse-riding stance. At the same time, twist the upper body to the left and

13	14 **11**	15 **12-14**	16

attack directly to the front with the right elbow, the back of the right fist upward, the palm of the left hand remaining against the front of the right fist as shown in figure 15.

During this movement, the position of the head and the setting of the hips and legs must remain unchanged, in spite of the turning of the body to the left. Although Movements 11 and 12 are presented as two movements, they should be executed as a single motion. The point here is simultaneous attacks to the opponent's leg with the right foot and to his solar plexus with the right elbow.

13. Without altering the hips or legs, return the upper body to its earlier position (directed to the front) and face to the right. At the same time, open the right hand and execute a right middle level block to the right side while drawing the left fist back to the left hip, as shown in figure 16. The point here is to grasp an opponent's wrist as he attacks from the right. In the block, the right hand should be about at the level of the right shoulder.

14. Without altering the stance, clench the right fist and draw it back to

17	18 **15**	19	20 **16-20**

21   22   23   24

the right hip, fingers upward, at the same time positioning the left arm horizontally in front of the chest, fingers downward. The point here is to grasp an opponent's attacking arm and, while twisting it, draw it in to the right hip.

15. Without altering the posture or moving the right foot, cross the left foot lightly over the right.

16. Keeping the left foot in place, take a big step to the right with the right foot into a horse-riding stance. At the same time, face to the front and execute a middle level block directly to the front with the left forearm, rotating the left fist in the motion until the back of the fist is turned downward. The right fist is maintained at the right hip. The final position is that shown in figure 31 of Tekki Shodan.

17. Without changing the stance, swing the left fist across in front of the right shoulder and down into a left down block, at the same time starting the right fist from below and outside the left elbow and drawing it up into a middle level block.

18. Continuing the upward motion of the right fist, raise it above the right shoulder with the fingers directed toward the front and attack at face level to the front. At the same time, bring the left forearm into a horizontal position across the chest with the back of the fist upward and the left wrist just under the point of the right elbow.[36] Execute Movements 17 and 18 as a single movement. The movement is similar to that shown in Movements 27, 28 and 29 of Tekki Shodan.

19. Keeping both feet in place, simultaneously turn the head to face to the left, open the right hand and withdraw it to the right hip, palm inward, and place the left fist against the right palm. This is the mirror image of Movement 9.

20. Without changing the stance, execute a left middle level block with the left fist to the left side, rotating the fist until the fingers are upward, placing the

36. Customarily there is a kiai at this point in the kata. [Translator's note.]

right hand on the inside of the left forearm with the fingertips at the left wrist. This is the mirror image of Movement 10 (cf. figure 13). The right hand and left forearm are to remain in contact throughout the motion.

21. Without shifting the right foot, simultaneously turn the head to face directly to the front, raise the left knee up, and pull both hands back to the left hip, bringing the left fist to the hip, fingers upward, in a flowing motion and the right palm against it. This is the mirror image of the position shown in figure 14.

22. Stamping the left foot strongly into its former horse-riding stance, rotate the upper body to the right and attack to the front with the left elbow. The back of the left fist is turned upward and the right hand is positioned with the palm against the front of the left fist. This is the mirror image of the position shown in figure 15.

Movements 21 and 22 are mirror images of Movements 11 and 12, and the comments given there apply here as well. Movements 21 and 22 should be executed as a single movement.

23. Without altering the stance of the hips or legs, return the body to face directly to the front. At the same time, turn the head to the left, open the left hand to execute a middle level block to the left side, palm downward, and pull the right fist back to the right hip. This is the mirror image of figure 16.

24. Without changing the stance, draw the left fist in a twisting motion to the left hip, at the same time bringing the right forearm to a horizontal position in front of the chest. This is the mirror image of Movement 14 (see also figure 8 of Tekki Shodan).

25. Without moving either the upper body or the left leg, cross the right foot lightly over the left.

26. Holding the right foot in place, take a big step to the left with the left foot. At the same time, turn the head to face to the front and swing the right fist into a middle level block to the front, fingers upward, while holding the left fist at the hip. Refer to figure 11 of Tekki Shodan.

27. Without altering the stance, block with both fists, the right starting from

29   30   25   31   32   26–28

33   34   35   36

a position in front of the left shoulder and striking downward, the left starting beneath and in front of the right elbow and swinging outside the right forearm upward in a middle level block.

28. Without pausing, continue the upward swing of the left fist to a point above the left shoulder, then strike out immediately to the front at face level, at the same time placing the right forearm in a horizontal position in front of the chest, the back of the wrist lightly touching the point of the left elbow.[37]

Movements 27 and 28 are the mirror images of Movements 17 and 18 and

37. Customarily there is a kiai at this point in the kata. [Translator's note.]

TEKKI NIDAN 135

should be executed in a single, rapid motion. Details of the motions can be seen in Movements 27, 28 and 29 of Tekki Shodan.

Yame. This completes the kata. At the command "Yame," slowly draw the left foot in and return to the yōi position.

TEKKI SANDAN

This form consists of thirty-six movements and requires about one minute to complete. The line of movement is the straight line, as in Tekki Shodan and Nidan.

Yōi. Assume the natural stance with heels separated, holding the clenched fists naturally in front of the upper thighs and facing directly to the front. This is the same as the yōi stance of Heian Shodan.

1. Keeping the left foot in place, stamp to the right with the right foot into a horse-riding stance, executing a middle level block with the left fist, fingers upward, and drawing the right fist to the right hip (see figure 31 of Tekki Shodan).

2. Without altering the stance, strike downward with the left fist from a point in front of the right shoulder in a lower level block while bringing the right fist from outside the left elbow in a middle level block, the fists describing a ripping motion.

3. Without altering the stance, position the left forearm in a horizontal plane in front of the chest, palm downward, and drop the right forearm, palm inward, down next to the left, as shown in figure 5, with the right elbow touching the left wrist.

An opponent, having his lower and middle level attacks blocked in Movement 2, retracts his fists and attacks again immediately with a double-hand technique. His left fist is blocked downward with the left hand and his right arm is deflected with the right wrist.

1   2   3   1-8   4

136   THE KATA

5   6   7   8

4. Without altering the stance or the position of the left arm, bring the right up to the upper level on the right side (see figure 6).

Finding his left fist deflected and his right fist knocked aside, the determined opponent relentlessly retracts his left fist and attacks once again; it is this attack being blocked here, the opponent's left wrist being hooked by the right wrist.

5. Without altering the stance or the position of the left arm, attack to the upper level with the right back fist in such a way that the right elbow comes to touch the upper surface of the left wrist (see figure 7). The right fist should be centered in front at slightly lower than eye level. The target is the opponent's philtrum. After learning them well, Movements 3 through 5 should be executed as a continuous, rapid unit.

6. Without altering the stance, draw the right fist back to the right hip (with fingers upward), open the left hand, holding the fingers together and thumb

9   10   11   9   12   10–17

TEKKI SANDAN 137

13   14   15   16

down, and position the palm of the left hand lightly on the inner surface of the right wrist.[38]

7. Without altering the stance, attack to the midline in front with the right fist, moving the left hand along with the rotating right hand, so that the left palm comes to rest at the completion of the attack on top of the right elbow. After learning them well, Movements 6 and 7 should be executed as a rapid unit.

8. Turning the head to face to the right, rotate the right fist to direct the palm upward while leaving the left hand at the same position on the right arm.

9. Without altering the posture, pass the left foot lightly over the right. The bending of the right leg is to be maintained during the motion and care taken that the torso not be tilted forward.

10. Keeping the left foot in place, stamp to the right with the right foot into a horse-riding stance, push the right arm outward to the right, continuing to hold the left hand in its position at the right elbow as shown in figure 12. The movement blocks a middle level attack from the right.

11. Without altering the stance, again rotate the right fist to direct the palm downward, and simultaneously, holding the left hand in its position at the right elbow throughout, describe a complete circle with the extended right arm, the right shoulder as its center, the hand passing downward to the left, then to the upper left section, over the forehead, and downward, as shown in figure 16. An opponent's kick to the open right side of the body is blocked by hooking his leg with the radial edge of the right wrist.

12. Without altering the stance, draw the right fist back to the right hip, fingers upward, at the same time sliding the left palm smoothly along the right forearm to rest it on the inside surface of the right wrist[39] at the right hip and turning the head to face to the front.

38. "Wrist" is not accurate for customary practice. Now, the fingers of one hand are placed on the other hand. [Translator's note.]
39. See note 38.

17   18   19   20

13. Without altering the stance, thrust the right fist out to the midline in front, palm downward, while sliding the left palm smoothly along the upper surface of the right forearm to rest it on the right elbow.

14. Without changing the stance, rotate the right fist, directing the palm upward, to execute a middle level block, at the same time thrusting the left fist downward in a lower level block, palm downward.

15. Without altering the stance, simultaneously execute a middle level block with the left fist, in a motion beginning outside the right elbow, and a lower level block with the right fist, in a motion beginning in front of the left shoulder and passing downward. The simultaneous execution of these two techniques brings the hands apart in a ripping motion, as shown in figure 22 and reverses the blocking roles of the two arms in Movement 14.

16. Without altering the stance, draw the left fist back and upward over the left shoulder and instantly attack forward to the upper section (a back fist attack to the opponent's philtrum), while at the same time positioning the right

21   22   23   24

25   26   **18**   27   28   **19–25**

29   30   31   32

forearm in a horizontal plane in front of the chest. The fists remain clenched and the palm downward, so that the left elbow rests lightly on the right wrist.[40] Movements 15 and 16 should be executed as a single, sudden unit after they have been well learned.

17. Without altering the stance or the posture, turn the head to face to the left.

18. Without altering the posture of the trunk or head and without moving the left foot, cross the right foot smoothly over the left.

40. Customarily there is a kiai at this point in the kata. [Translator's note.]

140 THE KATA

19. Without moving the arms or the right foot, step to the left with a strong stamping motion of the left foot, at the same time turning the head to face to the front.

20. Without altering the stance, bring the left fist down to the right arm. This position is the mirror image of that shown in figure 5. The point here is to strike aside an opponent's middle level attack with the left wrist.

21. Without altering the stance, draw the left fist back to the left upper section in a motion that is the mirror image of that shown in figure 6. The purpose here is to block to the left a second attack from the opponent.

22. Without altering the stance, attack toward the midline in front with the back fist. This is the mirror image of the attack shown in figure 7. After learning them well, Movements 20 through 22 should be executed as a continuous rapid unit.

23. Without altering the stance, draw the left fist back to the left hip, palm up, open the right hand, with the thumb down, and place the right palm on the inner surface of the left wrist.[41]

24. Without altering the stance, attack to the front with the left fist, palm downward, sliding the right palm smoothly along the left forearm to the elbow.

25. Without altering the stance or the position of the right hand, rotate the left fist, directing the fingers upward, while turning the head to face to the left.

26. Without altering the position of the body or left leg, pass the right foot smoothly over the left.

27. Without moving the right foot, stamp to the left with the left foot into a horse-riding stance and swing the arms out to the left, holding the right hand in place at the left elbow. This is the mirror image of the motion shown in figure 12.

28. Without altering the stance, rotate the left fist, directing the fingers downward, and describe a large circle with the left arm passing to the right side

41. See note 38.

37 38 39 40

41 42 43 44

and over the forehead, the right hand being maintained at the left elbow. This is the mirror image of the motion shown in figure 16.

29. Without altering the stance, draw the left fist back to the left hip while sliding the right palm smoothly down the left forearm to the wrist[42] and turning the head to face directly forward.

30. Without altering the stance, attack to the front with the left fist, fingers downward, sliding the right palm smoothly up the left forearm to the elbow.

---

42. See note 38.

31. Without altering the stance, simultaneously turn the head to face to the right, open the right hand and move the right arm to the right side as if catching an opponent's fist attack, at the same time pulling the left fist back to the left hip. This is the same position as that shown in figure 16 of Tekki Nidan.

32. Without altering the stance, simultaneously draw the right fist to the hip in a twisting motion and position the left arm in a horizontal plane in front of the chest with palm downward. This position is that shown in figure 28 of Tekki Shodan.

33. Without altering the posture of the body or moving the right foot, pass the left foot lightly over the right.

34. Without moving the left foot or the right fist, take a stamping step to the right side with the right foot into a horse-riding stance while simultaneously executing a middle level block with the left fist and turning the head to face directly to the front.

35. Without altering the stance, simultaneously execute a middle level block with the right fist in a motion starting ouside the left elbow and a lower level block with the left fist, the motion passing downward from in front of the right shoulder in a ripping motion of the hands.

36. Without altering the stance, draw the right fist back over the right shoulder, with fingers forward and instantly attack forward with the back fist to the upper section, at the same time positioning the left forearm in a horizontal plane in front of the chest with the fist clenched and fingers downward. The right elbow is touching the left wrist.[43] Movements 35 and 36 should be executed as a rapid single unit.

Yame. Without moving the left foot, draw the right foot smoothly in to it, straighten the legs, and slowly drop the fists to return to the yōi position.

HANGETSU

This kata consists of forty-one movements and takes about one minute to complete. The line of movement is the cross.[44]

Yōi. The stance is the natural stance with heels separated, the fists being held comfortably in front of the thighs. This is the same as the yōi stance of Heian Shodan.

1   2   3   1, 2   4

43. Customarily there is a kiai at this point in the kata. [Translator's note.]
44. Originally the numbering of the embu sen in Hangetsu was reversed. However we have changed it to conform with the other kata in the interest of continuity. [Translator's note.]

5　　　　　　　　　　　　6

7　　**3, 4**　　　　　　8　　　　　　　　9　　　　　　10　　**5–10**

1. Keeping the right foot in place, step forward with the left foot (front stance)[45] onto Line 2, sliding the foot in a crescent-shaped arc as shown in figure 2, at the same time executing a middle level block with the left fist, bringing it up from the right side in a large semicircular motion, and retracting the right fist to the right hip, fingers of both fists upward.

This form is of the Shōrei school, which stresses in particular the training and development of the body. These movements are executed slowly and display application of power at the critical points of each technique. This fact should be kept in mind during the form, especially in the manner of application of strength and in the tensing of the legs.

2. Without altering the stance, slowly pull the left fist back to the hip and extend the right fist toward the front.

3. Keeping the left foot in place, step forward onto Line 2 into a front stance with the right foot describing a crescent-shaped path and execute a middle level block to the front with the right fist, bringing it in a semicircular motion

45. In the latest edition, the word *zenkutsu* (front) was eliminated, because this front stance is not like the front stance in the other forms. The stance now used in this form is called the half-moon stance (*hangetsu-dachi*). [Translator's note.]

past the front of the left shoulder in a motion that is the mirror image of Movement 1.

4. Without altering the stance, draw the right fist back to the hip and extend the left fist toward the front.

5. Keeping the right foot in place, slide the left foot forward along Line 2 in a crescent-shaped arc into a front stance, at the same time executing a middle level block with the left fist in a large semicircular motion passing in front of the right shoulder, and withdraw the right fist to the hip. This movement is similar to Movement 1 (cf. figure 3).

6. Without altering the stance, extend the right fist toward the front, at the same time pulling the left fist back to the hip. This is identical to Movement 2.

7. Without altering the stance, form both fists into index finger single-point fists and slowly draw them to points just below the nipples, palms downward, from their final positions in the preceding movement. Raise and extend the elbows to the sides and lower the shoulders.

8. Without altering the stance, extend both fists (still in single-point fists) toward the front with palms downward. The fists are held at shoulder width.

9. Without altering the stance, open both fists to four-finger spear hands, with palms facing each other, then pull the arms slowly backward to either side of the head, bending the elbows as necessary. In their final positions, the upper arms are level with the shoulders, the elbows bent at right angles, so that the arms and head together form a figure suggestive of the character for mountain (山). The chest is expanded. This posture, because of the positions of the arms, is called the mountain posture (*yamagamae*). It is an upper level block with both arms.

10. Without altering the stance, straighten the arms and lower them to the sides, the palms turned inward toward the thighs.[46] The position is that of a lower level block with both arms.

---

46. It is customary to cross the arms in front of the body while lowering them to the sides. [Translator's note.]

15   16   17   18

19   11, 12   20   21   22

11. Keeping the left foot in place, step forward with the right foot and then turn counterclockwise to the rear into a front stance,[47] at the same time executing a middle level block with the right hand, palm upward, in a motion proceeding from outside the left elbow and a lower level block with the left hand, palm downward, starting in front of the right shoulder, the hands describing a ripping motion. The final position is shown in figure 19. The movement is to be executed very quickly. Both hands are to be held with the index fingers straightened,

47. Customarily there is a kiai at this point in the kata. [Translator's note.]

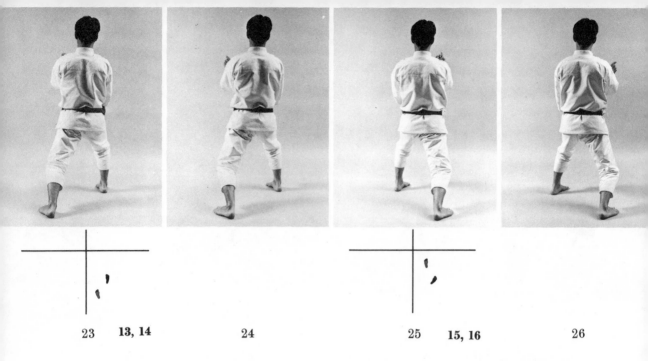

23   **13, 14**   24   25   **15, 16**   26

the remaining fingers and thumbs bent at the first joints. In the final position the hands are spaced shoulder width, i.e., the right hand is held in front of the right shoulder, the left in front of the left thigh.

12. Without altering the stance, slowly rotate the right wrist to direct the palm downward in a strong motion. During the motion, the right forearm should be depressed and drawn inward slightly toward the body. The point of the movement is first to block an opponent's middle level fist attack, then to rotate one's hand, catch the attacker's wrist, and draw him inward.

13. Keeping the left foot in place, step forward into a front stance, toward the rear of Line 2, and execute a lower level block with the right hand, palm downward, beginning in front of the left shoulder, and a middle level block with the left hand, beginning outside the right elbow, the hands being held as described in Movement 12 and moving together in a ripping motion. The final position is the mirror image of that shown in figure 19. Throughout the movements apply strength at crucial points.

14. Without altering the stance, slowly rotate the left wrist directing the palm downward. This is the mirror image of Movement 12.

15. Keeping the right foot in place, step forward (toward the rear of Line 2) with the left foot into the position shown in figure 25. The final stance and motion of the hands are identical to those in Movement 11. The meanings and notes given above apply here as well. Movements 11 through 16 are a threefold repetition of a pair of motions.

16. Without altering the stance, slowly rotate the right wrist directing the palm downward.

17. Pivoting on the left foot (it should be located on the intersection of Lines 1 and 2), step out toward the right with the right foot into a front stance (i.e., onto the left branch of Line 1), at the same time turning the head to face to the right and executing a middle level forearm block with the right fist, the left fist being withdrawn with fingers upward to the left hip. Movement 17 is to be performed very quickly.

148   THE KATA

27   28 **17–19**   29   30

18. Without altering the stance, draw the right fist back to the right hip (with fingers upward) and thrust outward with the left fist in a middle level attack.

19. Without altering the stance, draw the left fist back to the hip, simultaneously executing a middle level attack with the right fist. Movements 18 and 19 are to be executed in a continuous, rapid motion (renzuki).

20. Pivoting with the feet in place, turn counterclockwise to face along the right branch of Line 1 (i.e., in the direction opposite to that of Movement 17), then advance along Line 1 in a sliding (yori-ashi) motion into a front stance and execute a middle level block with the left fist, fingers upward, pulling the right fist back to the right hip; this movement is the mirror image of Movement 17.

With respect to the sliding technique, see the explanation of figure 50 of Heian Sandan. With the feet in the position described in Movement 19 and the right foot propelling the sliding motion, the body turns naturally to face in the direction of motion.

31   32 **20–22**   33   34

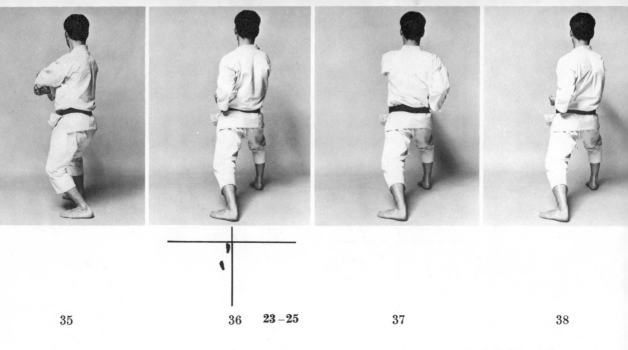

35   36   **23–25**   37   38

21. Without altering the stance, draw the left fist back to the left hip and simultaneously execute a middle level attack with the right fist.

22. Without altering the stance, draw the right fist back, at the same time executing a middle level attack with the left fist. Like Movements 18 and 19, 21 and 22 are to be executed as a single, continuous motion (renzuki).

23. Pivoting with the left foot in place, turn 90 degrees to face toward the rear of Line 2, the right foot describing a crescent-shaped arc. The motion is better executed with a slight feeling of a sliding movement. Execute a middle level block with the right fist, while drawing the left fist back to the hip. The movement is similar to Movement 17.

24. Without altering the stance, execute a middle level attack with the left fist while drawing the right fist to the hip.

25. Without altering the stance, execute a middle level attack with the right fist, drawing the left fist back to the hip. Movements 24 and 25 are to be executed in rapid succession, i.e., renzuki.

26. Pivoting on the right foot, draw the left foot to the right and upward in a large arc. Turning to the rear (i.e., toward the front of Line 2), assume a horse-riding stance,[48] placing the left foot onto Line 2; at the same time, draw the left fist toward the right to execute a left back fist attack toward the front in the final position, as shown in figure 43. The eyes should be fixed on the left fist. The large circular motion of the left foot and fist should be executed slowly and without interruption even as contact is made with the right leg and fist. At the focal moment of the motions, strength should be applied to the fist, the foot, and to the lower abdomen, the feeling being that of an attack to an opponent's hand with the left back fist.

27. Without altering the posture of the body, step toward the front of Line 2, crossing the right foot lightly over the left. An opponent having grasped the left fist with his right hand and proceeding to draw it toward him, one moves to close up the distance.

48. In the latest edition, this is a back stance. [Translator's note.]

150 THE KATA

39   40   41   42

43 **26**   44   45 **27** 46

28. Without moving the right foot, kick upward in front of the left fist, at the same time drawing the latter back to a point in front of the right shoulder. Kicking the opponent's right arm, one frees and withdraws his left fist.

29. Lower the left foot onto Line 2 to assume a horse-riding stance,[49] at the same time thrusting the left fist outward toward the left, along Line 2, in a middle level attack, fingers downward. During the execution of this movement, both chest and abdomen are directed along the right branch of Line 1, with only

---

49. In the latest edition, this stance is the immovable. [Translator's note.]

47   **28**   48   49

the face turned toward the left. A slight feeling of a sliding movement should accompany the attack.

30. Pulling the left fist back to the left hip, twist the body to the left and thrust the right fist outward in a middle level reverse punch to the left side, at the same time changing to a front stance by bending the left knee without altering the positions of the feet. Having freed the left fist from an opponent's grip with a left kick to his right arm, one follows immediately with a left-right continuous attack (renzuki).

31. Without altering the stance, execute a left upper level rising block (cf. figure 12 of Heian Shodan). Movements 28 to 31 should be executed rapidly as a unit once they have been learned well.

32. Pivoting on the left foot and drawing the left fist to the hip, turn to face to the rear (i.e., toward the back of Line 2) while simultaneously drawing the right fist toward the left fist to execute a right back fist attack and drawing the right foot to the left, swinging it upward in a large arc, and placing it down onto

50   **29**   51   52   **30, 31**   53

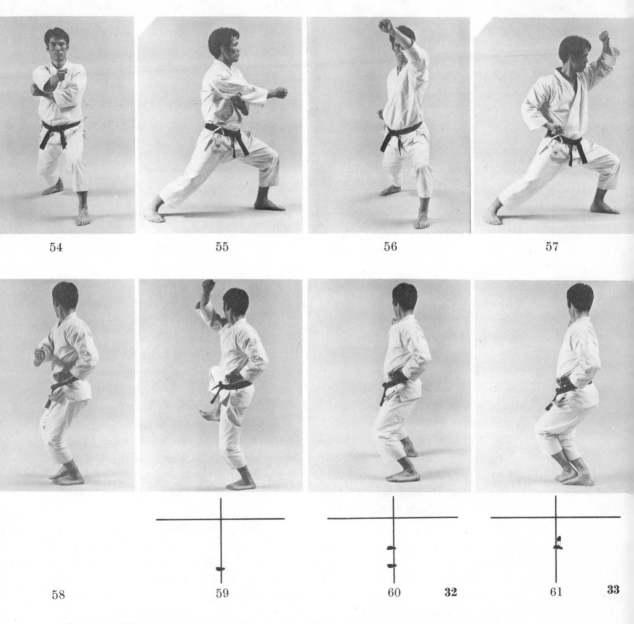

54   55   56   57

58   59   60 **32**   61 **33**

the rear of Line 2 in a horse-riding stance,[50] completing the motion as shown in figure 60. This movement is the mirror image of Movement 26.

33. Maintaining the posture of the body, move toward the rear of Line 2, crossing the left foot lightly over the right. This is the mirror image of Movement 27.

34. Without moving the left foot, kick upward with the right foot in front of the right fist and draw the latter back to the left shoulder. This movement is the mirror image of Movement 28.

---

50. In the latest edition, this is a back stance. [Translator's note.]

62   **34**   63   **35**   64   **36, 37**   65

35. Lower the right foot onto Line 2 in a horse-riding stance,[51] at the same time thrusting the right fist toward the right side in a middle level attack with fingers downward while holding the left fist at the left hip. This is the mirror image of Movement 29.

36. Pulling the right fist back to the right hip, twist the body to the right and thrust the left fist outward to the right side in a middle level reverse punch, at the same time changing to a front stance by bending the right knee and straightening the left without altering the position of the feet. This movement is the mirror image of Movement 30.

37. Without altering the stance, execute a right upper level rising block (cf. figure 16 of Heian Shodan, noting however the front stance here). During the movement, draw the left fist back to the left hip. This is the mirror image of Movement 31. Movements 34 to 37 should be executed as a rapid unit once they have been learned well.

38. Pivoting on the right foot and drawing the right fist to the right hip, turn to face to the rear (i.e., toward the front of Line 2) while simultaneously drawing the left fist toward the right to execute a left back fist attack and drawing the left foot to the right, swinging it upward in a large arc, and placing it down onto the front of Line 2 in a horse-riding stance.[52] This movement is identical to Movement 26.

39. Without moving the left foot, open the left fist and swing the right foot in a semicircular arc toward the front to kick the extended left palm. This is the crescent-moon kick.

Refer to the descriptions of this kick in Movements 15 of Heian Godan and 27 of Bassai. The point here is to grasp the opponent while in the final position of Movement 38 and then to draw him inward and kick his chest with the right foot.

---

51. In the latest edition, this stance is the immovable. [Translator's note.]
52. In the latest edition, this is a back stance. [Translator's note.]

66   67   68

69   70   71   **38**   72

40. Keeping the left foot in place, lower the right foot to its former position to assume a front stance, at the same time twisting the body to the left and drawing the left fist back to the hip while executing a middle level attack with the right fist.[53] The right fist is to attack the same point in space previously occupied by the left hand. Movements 39 and 40 are to be executed in a single, rapid motion.

41. Keeping the right foot in place, draw the left foot in toward it to assume

<hr>

53. Customarily there is a kiai at this point in the kata. [Translator's note.]

73   74   **39**   75

76   **40**   77

a cat leg stance (*nekoashi-dachi*) and bring the hands together at the left knee in the position of a leg block (against a foot), as shown in figure 79.

As described in chapter 3, the cat leg stance requires the trunk to be upright, the weight resting on the bent right knee, and the left leg bent with the ball of the foot held lightly on the ground. This is a difficult stance requiring careful study of the illustration and practice.

Yame. Without moving the right foot, move the left foot out and return to the yōi stance.

78   79   **41**   80   81

JUTTE

There are twenty-four movements, taking about one minute to complete; the line of movement is the cross, i.e., the same as that of Hangetsu.

Yōi. The yōi stance is that shown in figure 2, the feet-together stance, with the right fist at a point eight to nine inches in front of the chin and the palm of the left hand covering the right fist. The elbows are slightly out, and the armpits slightly open.

1. Without moving the right foot, drop the left foot back to assume a front stance. Drawing the left fist slowly to the left hip, form the right hand into a shallow fist with the distal two joints of the fingers tightly flexed and rotate it slowly in a circle starting in front of the chest, passing upward by the chin, then outward to the front, and finally downward to execute a middle level downward pressing block (*osai-uke*) with the palm upward. In this movement, the wrist of the opponent is deflected downward by the block with the right wrist. The final position is similar to that shown in figure 55 for Empi except that in the present case the left fist is brought to the left hip. The shallow fist described for the right hand is characteristic of this kata, being contained in each of Movements 1 through 7, so that it should be practiced with diligence.

2. Without moving the right foot, while stepping diagonally left to the front with the left foot onto the left branch of Line 1 into a front stance, flex the fingers and thumb to form a shallow fist of the left hand and raise it slowly, as if lifting a heavy object, into a middle level block, palm upward as shown in figure 7. At the same time, form the right fist as before and invert it, pressing downward in a middle level block. Note that the strength is to be focused in the tips of the fingers, and the hands should be at shoulder width. The point to the motion of the right hand is to hold an opponent's wrist down.

3. Without changing the positions of the legs or the right hand, drop the

JUTTE 157

1   2   3   4

5   **1**   6   7   **2, 3**   8

left forearm to the right in a horizontal position parallel to the plane of the chest with the palm downward, at the same time turning the head to face to the right.

Such movements as one through three are techniques used to attack the opponent's elbows or wrists and knock them away to the side by pushing down with the back of the hand or pushing up with the heel of the hand.

4. Without shifting the left foot, step with the right foot onto the right branch of Line 1 into a front stance, at the same time clenching the left fist and drawing it to the hip while executing a middle level block to the right with the right wrist, the hand clenched in a shallow fist.

158   THE KATA

5. Keeping the left foot and fist in place, pivot to the left to bring the right foot onto the forward branch of Line 2 into a horse-riding stance,[54] and swing the right hand inward toward the center from the right side as if hitting away, its fingers and thumb flexed into a shallow fist, the back of the fist toward the right side of Line 2, to execute a right middle level block. The right elbow should be slightly bent.

Following the block of an attack from the right side in Movement 4, the present technique is a block of a subsequent attack from the front in which one steps into the opponent and hits away the attack with the right palm. One should therefore be facing toward the front of Line 2.

6. Pivoting on the right foot, step forward along Line 2 with the left foot, assuming a horse-riding stance,[55] and at the same time draw the right fist to the hip and block inward toward the center from the left side with the left hand, its fingers and thumb flexed into a shallow fist. This is the mirror image of Movement 5. The technique is executed three times in Movements 5 through 7, and in each case the face is to be directed to the front, the body rotating to face to the left or right of Line 2 depending on the position of the legs (i.e., from left to right to left, respectively, in the three movements).

7. Pivoting on the left foot, step forward along Line 2 with the right foot into a horse-riding stance,[56] at the same time drawing the left fist back to the hip and blocking toward the center from the right side at middle level with the right hand, its fingers and thumb flexed into a shallow fist. This is identical to Movement 5.

8. Without moving the left foot, cross the right leg in front of the left, at the same time raising the fists and crossing them in front of the forehead, the right

54. Movement 5 is customarily initiated by drawing the left foot in to Line 2 rather than by holding the foot in place. In the latest edition, this stance is the immovable. [Translator's note.]

55. In the latest edition, this stance is the immovable. [Translator's note.]

56. In the latest edition, this stance is the immovable. Customarily there is a kiai at this point in the kata. [Translator's note.]

13   7   14   8   15

outside the left. The face and body are directed toward the left side of Line 2.

Having blocked an attack coming from the front of Line 2 in the previous movement, one now blocks an upper level attack from the left side with the crossed fists. The legs are crossed to protect the testicles in a stance similar to one occurring in Heian Godan.

9. Without moving the right foot, step to the side, (i.e., toward the rear of Line 2) with the left foot into a horse-riding stance, at the same time swinging the fists down to the sides, the backs of the fists directed outwards, the face directed to the left side of Line 2. The fists are positioned about six to seven inches from the thighs. The point of the technique is simultaneous blocks to both sides of fist or foot attacks to the sides of the body.

10. Maintaining the horse-riding stance, shift both feet to the left (i.e., toward the back of Line 2) with the sliding technique, at the same time thrusting the fists upward to cross the forearms in front of the chest and then outward widely in a ripping motion to the two sides into the position shown in figure 19.

16   9   17   18   19

20   **10**   21   22   23

During the motion, continue to face to the left side of Line 2. Note: this stance, called the mountain posture (yamagamae) because of the resemblance of the configuration of the head in the center and the two fists at the sides to the character for mountain (*yama*, 山), is also applied with the hands open, as, for example, in Hangetsu. The meaning of the motion is to force apart the two fists of an opponent at the front delivering a two-handed attack.

11. Facing to the right (i.e., toward the front of Line 2) and pivoting on the right foot, step forward along Line 2 with the left foot into the stance shown in figure 24, hitting in toward the center from the side with the left fist without altering the posture of the body or arms from the preceding movement. Throughout the block, the eyes are to be fixed on an opponent at the front of Line 2. The purpose here is to block an opponent's upper level attack by striking it out of the way with the left fist while simultaneously stamping down onto his instep with the left foot (*fumikomi*). In stepping in with the left foot, one is to support his weight on the right leg while drawing the left foot up to thigh level.

24   **11**   25   26

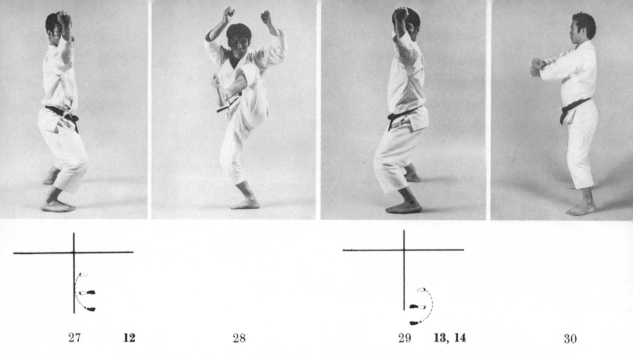

27   **12**   28   29   **13, 14**   30

12. Continuing to face toward an opponent to the front, pivot on the left foot and move in to attack to the front along Line 2 with the right fist and leg simultaneously while maintaining the posture of the body and shoulders from the preceding movement. Assume the mirror image of the stance shown in figure 24. The setting of the body and shoulders is the mountain posture, that of the hips and legs a horse-riding stance. This and Movement 13 are repetitions of the technique in Movement 11.

13. Continuing to face toward an opponent at the front, pivot on the right foot and move in to attack to the front along Line 2 with the left fist and foot, simultaneously maintaining the posture of the body and arms to assume the position shown in figure 29. This is identical to Movement 11.

14. Slowly lowering the fists, turn the head to face to the front (i.e., toward the right side of Line 2), and straighten the legs, keeping the feet in place, to assume a stance similar to the yōi stance of Heian Shodan, but with slightly wider separation of the feet.

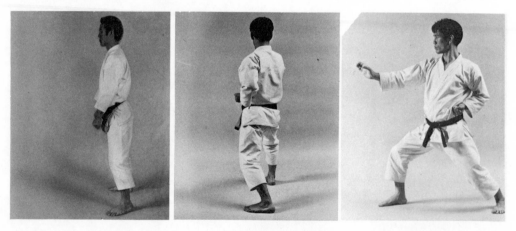

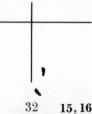

31   32   **15, 16**   33

34   35   36   37

15. Turning to the right and bending the right leg to assume a front stance, face toward the back of Line 2, open the right hand and swing it out toward the right, the back of the hand directed toward the right, the arm bent at the elbow, and withdraw the left fist to the hip. The right hand is placed as if it were about to grasp an object to the front. The position is similar to that shown in figure 16 for Tekki Nidan, except that the stance in the present kata is the front stance, rather than the horse-riding stance.

16. Maintaining the previous stance, lower the right hand without changing its form to a point six to seven inches over the right knee. At the same time, open the left hand into a form similar to that of the right, with fingers straightened and held together, palm directed to the right, and move it to the point in space occupied by the right hand at the beginning of this movement. The positions of the hands should define a vertical line. The point is to interrupt an

38   39   40

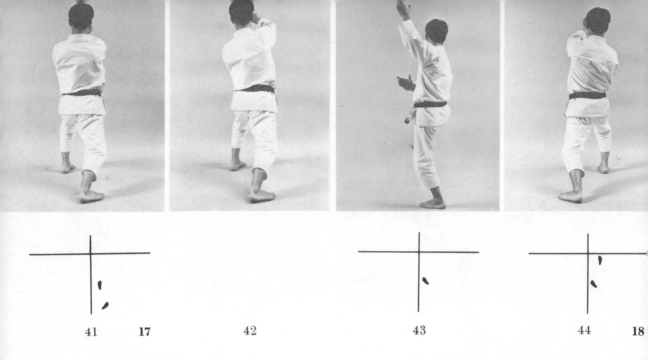

41　　**17**　　　　42　　　　　　43　　　　　　44　　**18**

attack with a stick at its start. Refer to the section on weapons and Karate-dō in the discussion of kumite.

17. Keeping the right foot in place, lift the left foot up to the position shown in figure 38, at the same time[57] raising the right hand high above the shoulder and bringing the left hand to the right side of the body. Without pausing, simultaneously step toward the front with the left foot to assume a front stance and push both hands forward to bring the left hand six to seven inches above the left knee and the right at shoulder level in a vertical line with the left hand. The hands are to remain open. The final position here is the mirror image of that in Movement 16. The point of the movement is to step in with the left leg onto an opponent's *sokei* region (area where the thigh meets the lower abdomen) while forcing away a stick held by him.

18. Keeping the left foot in place, bring the right foot up high, raise[58] the left hand high above the shoulder and draw the right hand to the left side to assume the mirror image of the position shown in figure 38, then step immediately toward the front with the right foot to assume a front stance and push both hands forward until the right is six to seven inches above the right knee and the left is at shoulder level in a vertical line above the left fist. This movement is a repetition of the technique in Movements 16 and 17.

19. Pivoting to the left on the right foot, step onto the left branch of Line 1, assuming a back stance, turning the head to face to the left side of Line 1, and execute an upper level block with the right fist, fingers toward the head, and a lower level block with the left fist, fingers downward. Lean slightly to the right. The right elbow is to be bent and the fist held at about the level of the head, while the left arm is straightened and the left fist held six to seven inches

57. Customarily, prior to reversing the vertical positions of the hands, one rotates each hand clockwise through 180 degrees about the forearms as axes, bringing the left palm to face to the left side, the right palm to the right. [Translator's note.]
58. Note 57 applies in this case as well, except that the initial rotation of the hands is counterclockwise. [Translator's note.]

164 THE KATA

45   46   **19**   47   48   **20**

49   50   51   52   **21**

over the thigh. This stance is the same as that in the last movement of Heian Godan and in Movement 19 of Kwankū.

20. Turning to the right with the feet in place, bending the left leg and straightening the right leg, assume a left back stance, face to the right, and execute an upper level block to the left side with the left fist and a lower level block to the right side with the right fist. This is the mirror image of Movement 19.

21. Keeping the right foot in place and stepping forward onto Line 2 with

53   **22**   54   55   **23**

56   **24**   57   58   59

the left leg after first straightening it,[59] execute an upper level block with the left fist, and withdraw the right fist to the hip. This is the same stance as that shown in figure 17 of Heian Shodan. In the present movement, the right fist is brought over the head prior to raising the left fist and is then retracted in such a way that the wrists pass through a crossed position, as discussed in detail with respect to Movement 9 of Heian Shodan.

59. Customarily, the straightening of the left leg and the right arm block are emphasized as follows: from the back stance of Movement 20, one straightens the legs sharply, drawing the feet toward each other, and executes a strong right rising block, retracting the left fist to the left hip. Subsequently, it has also become customary to use the front stance while executing the left rising block. [Translator's note.]

166 THE KATA

22. Without moving the left foot, step forward along Line 2 with the right foot, simultaneously draw the left fist back to the hip and raise the right fist to a position in front of the forehead. This is the mirror image of the final block in Movement 21. Refer to figure 19 of Heian Shodan.

23. Turning counterclockwise with the feet in place,[60] face to the back of Line 2 and execute an upper level block, bringing the left fist to a position in front of the forehead, at the same time drawing the right fist back to the hip.

24. Without moving the left foot, step forward with the right (i.e., toward the back of Line 2) and execute an upper level block with the right fist, at the same time drawing the left fist back to the hip. Note that the same technique is contained in each of Movements 21 through 24. Refer to the description of this technique in the discussion of Heian Shodan for greater detail about the motions of the fist and the stance.

Yame. Pivoting on the right foot, turn slowly counterclockwise, drawing the left foot to the right, and return to the yōi stance shown in Figure 58.

EMPI

There are thirty-seven movements, taking about one minute to complete. The line of movement is the T.

Yōi. Standing in the feet-together stance with the open left hand at the hip,

1   2   3   4   1

---

60. Customarily there is a kiai at this point in the kata. [Translator's note.]

5   2   6   3   7   4   8   5,

palm toward the body, hold the right fist, fingers inward, against the left palm, as shown in figure 2.

1. Pivoting on the right foot, step out onto the left branch of Line 1 with the left foot, kneeling, the right knee on the floor, and thrust downward in front of the right thigh with the right fist, fingers inward, while positioning the left forearm across the chest, fingers of the left fist upward, with the face turned to the right. Refer to figure 4. The point of this movement is to scoop the kicking leg of an opponent to the right with the right arm, take hold of him with the left hand, and throw him.

2. Continuing to face to the right, straighten up without shifting the feet, draw the left fist to the hip, fingers up, and place the right fist, fingers inward onto the left fist.

3. Without altering the position of the feet, execute a lower level block with the right fist. This is similar to the third movement of Heian Shodan.

4. Turning to the front and facing along Line 2 while straightening the right leg, forcefully draw the right fist to the hip in a twisting motion and thrust the left forearm across the chest into a horizontal position with the fist in front of the chest, fingers downward. The left wrist is about six inches from the chest.

5. Keeping the right foot in place, step forward along Line 2 with the left foot, at the same time executing a lower level block with the left fist. In order to impart initial momentum to the block, first bring the left fist upward to a point over the right shoulder and place the right hand forward under the left arm, and then thrust the left fist downward and draw the right fist back to the right hip. The parting of the two fists has the feeling of a ripping motion.

6. Without shifting the feet, pull the left fist to the hip and thrust the right fist directly forward in an upper level attack, turning the body slightly to the left. The motion of the right fist has the sense of an attack to the chin from underneath.

7. Opening the outstretched right fist, jump forward onto the right foot, drawing the left foot up to a position just behind the right heel, legs crossed.

168 THE KATA

9   10   11   12

Simultaneously, reclenching the right fist, draw it toward the left shoulder, as if grasping and pulling an opponent inward, and execute a lower level attack with the left fist as shown in figure 13. The target of the attack of the left fist is the lower abdomen.

8. Without shifting the right foot, step backward with the left foot into a back stance, at the same time drawing the left fist to the hip and extending the right fist to the front in a lower level block, separating the fists in a ripping motion. The eyes are to be directed to the front throughout.

In forcing an opponent to release a hold on the left forearm, one is here either pushing the opponent's hand away with the right hand or attacking the upper or lower surface of the wrist with the right iron hammer or wrist.

9. Turning counterclockwise with the feet in place, move naturally into a front stance and execute a left down block while withdrawing the right fist to the hip. The final posture is like that of Movement 1 of Heian Shodan.

10. Keeping the feet in place, draw the left fist back to the left hip and exe-

13   7   14   8   15   16   **9, 10**

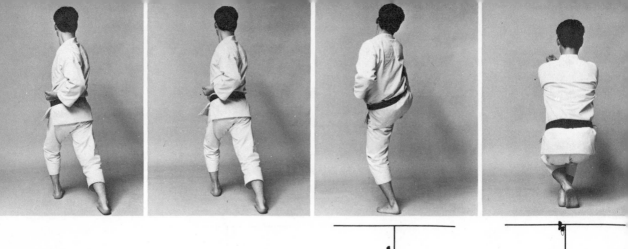

17   18   19   20   11

cute an upper level attack to the front with the right fist. This movement is the same as Movement 6.

11. Jumping inward toward the rear of Line 2 with the right foot and placing the left foot at the back of the right heel, clench the extended right fist and move it toward the front of the left shoulder as if drawing an opponent inward, at the same time executing a lower level attack with the left fist. This movement is the same as Movement 7 (see figure 13).

12. Stepping backward with the left foot into a left back stance, simultaneously draw the left fist back to the hip and execute a lower level block with the right fist. The wrists are crossed, the right fist being drawn along the upper side of the withdrawing left forearm. This movement is similar to Movement 8.

13. Turning counterclockwise with the feet in place to face toward the back (i.e., toward the front of Line 2), move naturally into a front stance, at the same time executing a lower level block with the left fist and drawing the right fist to the hip. This is similar to Movement 9.

21   **12**   22   **13**   23   24

25   26   14   27   28

14. Without moving the right foot, swing the opened left hand and left foot, in parallel paths, toward the left along the left branch of Line 1, bringing the left hand up to eye level, the foot moving so that a horse-riding stance is assumed. The eyes are to be fixed on the left hand throughout the movement. The open left hand comes to be extended diagonally to the front at eye level, the eyes still fixed on it.

15. Without moving the left hand or foot, first swing the right fist upward, fingers directed toward the front, then strike the left palm with the right forearm so that the tips of the fingers of the left hand come to the level of the right wrist, fingers of the right fist toward the back. During the motion, place the right instep against the back of the left knee, face to the front, and give a kiai, "Ei!"

16. Keeping the left foot in place, return the right foot to its position in Movement 14, assuming a horse-riding stance. Move the left palm to the right side of the body, as if gathering up a kimono sleeve, and simultaneously swing

29   **15**   30   31   32

33　**16–18**　　　　34　　　　　35　　　　　36

the right arm in a large clockwise circle past the forehead, down to the right, and in front to entrap an opponent's arm; then extend the left arm to the front in an open hand block, fingers together, thus blocking from the inside an opponent's middle level attack, while drawing the right forearm over the left to bring the right fist to the hip. Refer to Movement 5 of Kwankū.

17. Without altering the horse-riding stance, draw the extended left hand back to the hip while clenching the fist and executing a middle level attack with the right fist.

18. Without altering the stance, execute a middle level attack to the front with the left fist and withdraw the right fist to the hip. Movements 17 and 18 should be executed in rapid succession as a continuous attack.

19. Pivoting on the right foot, step onto the left branch of Line 1 with the left foot into a front stance and execute a down block toward the left side with the left fist, starting the block from a point in front of the right shoulder, at the

37　**19, 20**　　　　38　　　　　39　　**21**　　　40

41   **22, 23**   42   43   **24**   44

same time withdrawing the right fist to the hip from the right lower section. The movement is similar to Movement 1 of Heian Shodan.

20. Keeping the feet in place, execute an upper level attack with the right fist and withdraw the left fist to the left hip. The upper body is twisted slightly to the left during the motion.

21. Keeping the left foot in place, step forward onto the left branch of Line 1 with the right foot into a back stance, while executing a middle level sword hand block with the right hand.

22. Reverse the positions of the feet by bringing the right foot back in line with the left and then placing the left foot forward onto the left branch of Line 1 at the initial position of the right foot (right back stance), at the same time executing a middle level sword hand block with the left hand.

23. Keeping the feet in place, pull the left hand back to the hip while clenching the fist and simultaneously thrusting the right fist forward in a middle level attack.

45   **25, 26**   46   47   48

24. Keeping the left foot in place, step forward along the left branch of Line 1 with the right foot into a left back stance and execute a middle level sword hand block with the right hand.

25. With the feet in place, turn counterclockwise to face to the rear (i.e., toward the right branch of Line 1), at the same time executing a down block with the left fist from a front stance and withdrawing the right fist to the hip.

26. Without altering the stance, thrust the right fist forward and then upward to attack an opponent's chin from underneath, pulling the left fist back to the hip. At the completion of the motion, the upper body should be turned to the left with the left shoulder back.

27. Facing along the right branch of Line 1, jump forward onto the right foot, bringing the left foot forward to touch the back of the right heel. At the same time, open and then close the extended right hand, drawing it in to a point in front of the left upper arm as if grasping an object and pulling it inward, while simultaneously executing a lower level attack toward the lower abdomen of an opponent with the left fist. This movement is similar to Movement 7.

28. Stepping backward with the left foot toward the left branch of Line 1 into a back stance, draw the left fist to the hip while extending the right fist forward in a lower level block. This movement is similar to Movement 8.

29. Turning with the feet in place, face toward the left branch of Line 1, moving naturally into a front stance, and execute a left down block while retracting the right fist to the hip.

30. Keeping the feet in place and drawing the left fist back to the hip, push upward in a middle level block with the open right hand, the palm upward, fingertips bent, and wrist bent back. For the form of the right hand refer to figure 53.

31. Keeping the left foot in place, step forward onto Line 2 with the right foot into a front stance, at the same time blocking simultaneously upward with a pushing motion of the right palm and downward with the left palm, as shown in figure 55.

174 THE KATA

53   54   55   **31**   56

57   **32**   58   59   **33, 34**   60

32. Step forward with the left foot along Line 2 into a front stance, while pushing upward with the left palm and downward with the right palm, performing the mirror image of the motion shown in figure 55.

33. Stepping forward along Line 2 with the right foot, block simultaneously upward with the right palm and downward with the left, in the same manner as that shown in figure 55. Movements 31–33 are a threefold execution of a technique.[61] As pointed out previously, the second motion in such a series is to be performed lightly and the third with full force.

---

61. It is customary to do Movements 31, 32 and 33 slowly. [Translator's note.]

61   62   63   **35**   64

34. Keeping the feet in place, pull the hands past each other in a ripping motion, the left fist back to the hip from below and the right fist up in front of the left shoulder and then downward in a lower level block to the front along Line 2. The body should shift into a left back stance. The left shoulder is retracted so that the body is directed toward the left side of Line 2, with the face directed to the right along Line 2. The right fist is held about six inches above the right thigh.

35. Sliding forward along Line 2 in a yori-ashi motion, position the open right hand in front as shown in figure 63, with the palm upward, elbow rotated slightly inward to be almost touching the side of the body, at the same time bringing the left hand, palm upward, to a point eight to nine inches in front of and slightly above the forehead.

36. Leap backward off both feet, as high and as far as possible, along Line 2, turning counterclockwise through a full 360 degrees in the air, landing in a left back stance and executing a right middle level sword hand block at the moment

65   66   67   **36**   68   **37**

69   70

of landing. Give a kiai, "Ei," at the start of the leap. The point here is to block an opponent's upper level attack with the left hand and thrust the right hand between his thighs, then raise him up and throw him bodily toward the rear. Upon landing, both feet must touch the ground at the same instant.

37. Step backward along Line 2 with the right foot into a right back stance and execute a left middle level sword hand block.

Yame. Sliding the left foot back, slowly assume the yōi stance.

GANKAKU

There are forty-two movements, taking about one minute to complete. The line of movement is the straight line.

Yōi. Assuming the natural stance, with feet turned outward and heels apart,

1   2   3   1-4   4

| 5 | 6 | 7 |

place the fists at their natural level in front of the thighs. This stance is identical to the yōi stance of Heian Shodan.

1. Pulling the right foot back, simultaneously swing the right hand up from the thigh to a point in front of the left shoulder, placing it on the back of the left hand to assume the upper level side block position shown in figure 3. (NB: the customary position of the hands is shown in figures 5 and 6.)

2. Without altering the stance, draw the hands across to the right side of the body, changing their relative positions during the motion so that the palm of the left hand comes to rest on the inside surface of the right wrist to form a cross with the wrist. Refer to Movement 10 of Heian Godan.

3. Drawing the hands apart, attack to the front with the left fist and draw the right fist to the hip. Refer to Movement 11 of Heian Godan.

4. Execute a middle level reverse punch with the right fist, drawing the left fist to the left hip.

5. Pivoting on the left foot, turn counterclockwise through 360 degrees,

| 8 | 9 | 10 | 11 |

178 THE KATA

12   13   14

stamping with the right foot to execute a right lower level block to the back. The point of the motion is a block against a kicking attack to the buttocks from behind.

6. Keeping the feet in place, turn to face to the front (i.e., forward along the line of movement) to assume a front stance, and thrust the hands, with fingers straightened, the right wrist crossed inside the left, upward to a position in front of the forehead. Look intently from under the crossed forearms.

7. Without altering the stance, lower the hands to chest level while clenching the fists.

8. Facing to the front, execute a double kick (*nidan-geri*), first with the right foot, then the left, landing on both feet simultaneously in a front stance while thrusting the crossed fists downward, the right over the left, to a point seven or eight inches above the left knee in a lower level scissors block.

9. Pivoting on the right foot to the right (i.e., clockwise) through 180 degrees to face to the rear, assume a front stance while thrusting the still crossed fists

15 5   16   17 6, 7   18

19   20   21   22

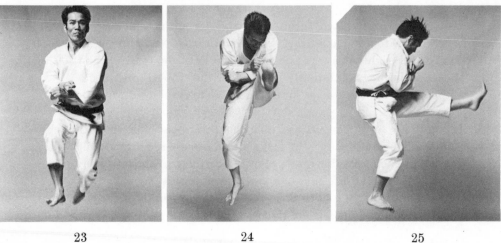

23   24   25

downward toward the left knee in a lower level scissors block. This block is the same as that in Movement 8.

10. Turning 180 degrees (clockwise) while keeping the feet in their same positions and assuming a left back stance, execute a right lower level block, fingers downward and position the left fist, fingers upward, in front of the body at waist level as shown in figure 32. The extended right forearm should be parallel to the right thigh.

11. Stepping forward with the left foot and assuming a right back stance, execute a lower level block to the front with the left sword hand, palm downward, placing the right sword hand, palm upward, in front of the abdomen,

26   8   27   28   29   9

30   31   32   10   33

with the fingertips about even with the left hip. Note that in blocks of this type it is always the case that the hand that is retracted (here, the right) crosses above the front (blocking) forearm.

12. While stepping forward with the right foot into a front stance, first raise both hands to a crossed position, the right inside the left, and then move them into the opening block position shown in figure 38.

13. Pivoting to the left with both feet in place, assume a horse-riding stance and again cross the wrists, the right inside the left, this time with the open

GANKAKU 181

34   35 | 11   36   37

38 | 12   39   40   41

palms directed toward the body; then move the hands into the middle level opening block position shown in figure 42.

14. Again cross the hands and then lower the hands to the sides, the arms extending slightly outward. At the same time, turn the head to face to the left (i.e., to the rear of Line 1) and straighten the body to its natural height.[62] Whenever the present motion of lowering the hands to the sides is executed, the feeling should be that of ripping an object and forcing the halves to one's sides.

---

62. It is customary to do Movements 11–14 slowly. [Translator's note.]

42   **13, 14**   43   44   45

15. With the feet in place, assume a right back stance and draw the hands apart, the left hand from in front of the right shoulder, the right from the lower left side, executing an upper level block to the right with the right fist and a lower level block with the left. The fists are to be clenched during the blocks. The final position is that shown in figure 43 for Heian Godan.

16. Keeping the left foot in place, step forward (toward the rear of the line of movement) with the right foot to assume a left back stance, facing along the line of movement with the trunk directed to the right side of the line (relative to the yōi position). At the same time, draw the fists apart in a ripping motion, the right above the left, the left fist starting from the lower right side, the right from in front of the left shoulder, to execute an upper level block with the left fist and a lower level block with the right.

17. Pivoting on the right foot, turn counterclockwise through 180 degrees to step forward (toward the rear of the line of movement) with the left foot and assume a right back stance. At the same time, bring the arms across the front

46   47   **15**   48   49   **16**

50   **17**   51   52   **18**   53

54   55   **19–21**   56   57

of the body, then draw them apart, the right from the lower left side into a right upper level block, the left fist from in front of the right shoulder down into a lower level block.

18. Shifting toward the rear of the line of movement, drop the right foot back into the area to the right of the line of movement, kneel on the right knee, with the left knee bent, and face toward the left side of the line of movement, concentrating the eyes on those of the opponent. At the same time, cross the wrists,

184 THE KATA

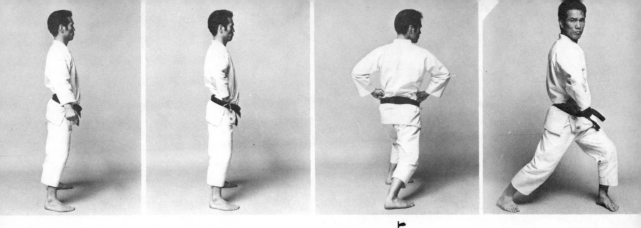

58   59   60   **22**   61

62   **23**   63   64   **24**

the right above the left, in a scissors block against an opponent's foot attack, as shown in figure 52.[63]

19. Raise the hips, bringing the right foot back onto the line of movement, assume a horse-riding stance while executing a middle level opening block. In blocking, the fists should cross, the right above the left, in a motion that overcomes their initial inertia.

20. Raise the hips to normal height, cross the wrists again in an opening block technique and lower the fists slowly to the sides.

63. Customarily there is a kiai at this point in the kata. [Translator's note.]

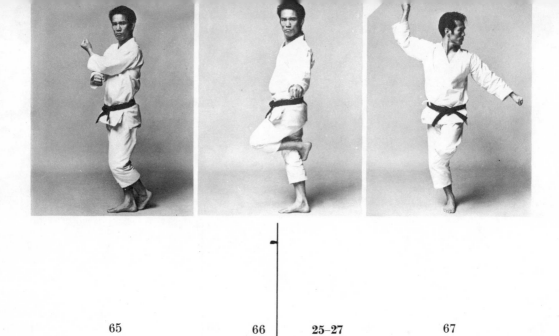

65   66 | 25–27   67

21. Bring both fists to the hips, the fingers directed to the back and the elbows extending out to the sides (arms akimbo).

22. Bending the left knee while holding the right knee straight, rotate the body to the left and attack to the front with the right elbow. The eyes are to remain fixed on those of the opponent.

23. Bending the right knee while straightening the left, rotate the body to the right and execute a left elbow attack against an opponent to the front. This is the mirror image of the preceding movement.

24. Pivoting on the right foot to the right through 180 degrees without raising the level of the hips, execute a middle level opening block, the backs of the fists directed forward, crossing the left foot behind the right and resting it with its outside edge against the right side of the right heel.

25. Bringing the arms across the body, the left hand in front of the right shoulder, the right at the lower left side, draw the arms apart, executing a lower level block with the left fist and an upper level block with the right, at the same time looking at an opponent to the left and placing the instep of the left foot on the back surface of the right knee, as shown in figure 66.

The name of this kata, Gankaku (crane on a rock), is derived from this one-footed stance, which resembles that of the crane.

26. Continuing to stand on the one foot, draw the right fist to the right hip, fingers upward, and place the left fist on top of the right, fingers inward, continuing throughout the motion to face toward an opponent to the left and maintaining eye contact with him.

27. Simultaneously attack with the back of the left fist and kick with the left sword foot (sokutō). The target of the fist attack is the upper jaw of the opponent, that of the left side-kick, his abdomen.

28. Returning the left foot to the ground, draw the left fist to the left hip and stepping forward with the right foot, execute a middle level right front punch to the left side (i.e., toward the front of the line of movement). After learning

186   THE KATA

68 69 70 71

them well, one should execute Movements 27 and 28 as a single, continuous motion.

29. Standing on the left foot with the instep of the right foot on the back of the left knee, cross the left hand to the lower right side and the right hand to a position in front of the left shoulder. Draw the fists apart in a ripping motion, executing an upper level block with the left fist and a lower level block with the right, while gazing into an opponent's eyes. This final stance is the mirror image of that shown in figure 66. The trunk is directed toward the left side of the line of movement.

30. Without altering the preceding stance, place the fists, the right over the left, at the left hip. This movement is the mirror image of Movement 26.

31. Simultaneously attack with the right back fist and kick with the right sword foot. This is the mirror image of Movement 27.

32. Lower the right foot into a horse-riding stance and immediately attack

72   28   73   29–31   74   75

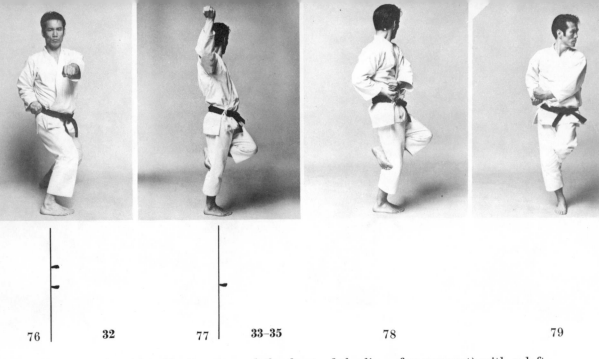

76   **32**   77   **33–35**   78   79

to the right side (i.e., toward the front of the line of movement) with a left middle level reverse punch, drawing the right fist to the right hip.

33. Turning to the left to face toward the rear of the line of movement, place the left foot on the back of the right knee. At the same time, bring the arms across the front of the body, then raise the right fist in an upper level block and drop the left to a lower level block. This is similar to Movement 25.

34. Without altering the stance, place the left fist on the right at the right hip.

35. Simultaneously attack with the back of the left fist and the left sword foot.

36. As the left foot touches the ground, draw the left fist to the left hip and attack toward the left side (i.e., toward the rear of the line of movement) with a right middle level reverse punch.

37. Without altering the stance, turn the head to face to the right (i.e., toward the front of the line of movement), at the same time executing a middle

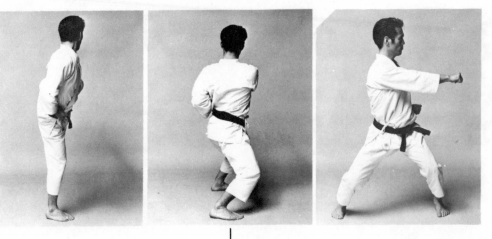

80   81   **36–39**   82

83   84   85   86

level block with the right hand, the fingers together, the palm toward the front, as if grasping an object (cf. Movement 13 of Tekki Nidan).

38. Without altering the stance, twist the upper body to the right and attack to the right side (i.e., forward along the line of movement) with the left elbow, the forearm being held in a vertical plane, while striking the front portion of the elbow with the right hand. The left elbow should be about six inches from the chest at the moment of contact with the right hand.

39. Without altering the stance, draw the open left hand back to the left hip with the palm turned upward, place the right fist onto the palm, fingers inward, while continuing to face to the right.

40. Pivot to the right through 360 degrees on the right foot. During the turn, raise the arms in front to bring the open hands up over the head, the fingers of the left over those of the right, then lower them, clenching the fists, to draw the right fist to the right hip, fingers upward, and the left onto the right, fingers inward. The motion of the hands should end at the instant of completion of the

87   88   89   90

91   **40, 41**   92   93   **42**   94

turn, and the head should be turned to face to the left (i.e., backward along the line of movement).

41. Simultaneously attack with the back of the left fist and with the left sword foot.[64]

42. As the left foot touches the ground, draw the left fist back to the left hip and execute a right middle level front attack, stepping into the attack with the right foot.

Yame. Pivot to the left on the right foot to return to the yōi position.

JION

There are forty-seven movements, taking approximately one and a half minutes to complete. The line of movement is the I.

Yōi. The stance here is similar to that of Jutte, the feet together and the right fist covered with the left hand. The position of the fists is out to the front and slightly below eye level.

1. Step back with the left foot to assume a front stance. Simultaneously with this movement, block downward with the left fist and perform a middle level forearm block with the right fist, the two fists moving in a ripping fashion, the left beginning from in front of the right shoulder and swinging downward, the right from in front of the left thigh and swinging upward.

2. Step diagonally forward to the left with the left foot. During this motion, cross the fists in front of the chest, with the right wrist inside the left, and assume the middle level opening block posture.[65] Note that in the opening block motion the hands may be formed either into fists (as here) or into the sword hand, with the palms in either case facing either to the front or towards the body. In all four cases, it should be observed, however, that the hands are to be held at about shoulder width from each other.

---

64. Customarily there is a kiai at this point in the kata. [Translator's note.]
65. This movement is customarily performed slowly. [Translator's note.]

190 THE KATA

3. Without moving the left foot, kick high between the fists with the right foot.

4. Stamping down strongly with the right foot, simultaneously execute a middle level attack to an opponent's chest with the right fist.

5. Without shifting the feet, retract the right fist and perform a middle level attack with the left fist.

6. Without moving the feet, execute a middle level attack with the right fist, retracting the left fist. After Movements 5 and 6 have been thoroughly practiced, they should be executed as a continuous motion. One should remem-

9 2

10 3

11 4–6

12

13

14

15 7

16 8

ber that the retracted fist, be it the left or the right, should always be poised for attack.

7. Holding the left foot in place, step diagonally to the right[66] with the right foot into a front stance. At the same time, first cross the fists, the right inside the left, and then draw them into a middle level opening block position.[67]

8. Kick high between the two fists with the left foot.

9. Keeping the right foot in place, stamp down strongly with the left foot,

66. This step is diagonally right from Line 2. [Translator's note.]
67. This movement is customarily performed slowly. [Translator's note.]

17   **9–11**   18   19   20

lowering it from the kick of Movement 8, simultaneously retracting the right fist and performing a middle level attack with the left fist.

10. Without moving the feet, retract the left fist and execute a middle level attack with the right fist.

11. Without moving the feet, retract the right fist and perform a middle level attack with the left fist. After thorough practice, Movements 10 and 11 should be executed as a continuous movement. Movements 2 to 11 bear some similarity to the continuous attack movements in Heian Yodan.

12. Keeping the right foot in place, step with the left foot to the left onto Line 2. During this motion, raise the right hand over the forehead with the palm facing to the front, then pull it down while raising the left fist in an upper level block similar to that in Heian Shodan. This movement also reflects that of the Heian form in its momentary crossing of the arms and ripping motion of the fists.

21   22   **12, 13**   23   24

25   26 **14, 15**   27   28

13. Keeping the feet in place, retract the left fist to the left hip and perform a middle level attack with the right fist.

14. While stepping forward with the right foot, first raise the left hand over the forehead, with the palm facing to the front, then retract it to the left hip, clenching the fist in the process, and simultaneously thrust the right fist upward in an upper level block. In this movement, which is similar to the upper level block in Heian Shodan, the termination of motion of the fists and feet should coincide.

15. Without moving the feet, retract the right fist to the right hip while executing a middle level attack with the left fist.

16. Stepping forward with the left foot, simultaneously raise the right hand with the palm forward in an upper level rising block, then retract the right hand from in front of the forehead to the right hip and raise the left fist upward in an upper level block. This movement is similar to the upper level block in Heian Shodan.

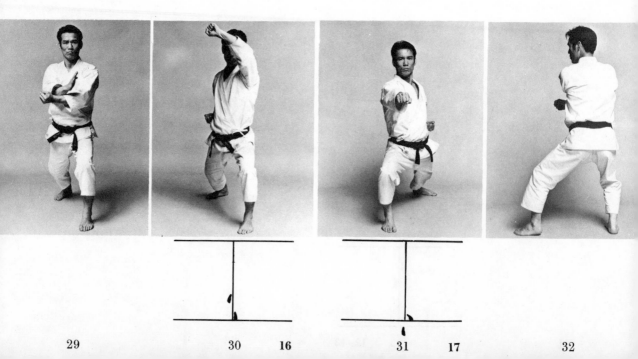

29   30 **16**   31 **17**   32

17. Step forward with the right foot, simultaneously executing a middle level attack with the right fist and retracting the left fist to the left hip.[68]

18. Keeping the right foot in place, pivot counterclockwise to step onto Line 3 with the left foot (assuming a back stance), simultaneously blocking with both fists in a ripping motion. The right fist starts below and under the left arm and rises to an upper level block; the left fist, with palm upward starts in front of the right shoulder and blocks downward in a lower level block.

19. Changing to a horse-riding stance with a sliding movement to the left, look to the left and retract the left fist to the left hip in a twisting motion and position the right fist, with fingers downward, in front of the solar plexus, with the forearm parallel to the body and about six inches in front of it.

20. Keeping the left foot in place, face to the right onto the left branch of Line 3 and assume a back stance. At the same time, in a ripping motion of the hands, block downward with the right fist in a motion starting from in front of the left shoulder and raise the left fist from below the right arm to execute an upper level block.

21. With a sliding motion to the right, retract the right fist to the right hip with a twisting action and simultaneously thrust to the right with the left fist in a motion bringing the left forearm into a horizontal position parallel to the plane of the chest and about six inches in front of it.[69] Refer to the same movement in Tekki Shodan. This movement is the mirror image of Movement 19.

22. Holding the right foot in place, step forward along Line 2 with the left foot, retract the right fist, passing under the left arm, to the right hip, and swing the left fist downward in a ripping motion from outside the right shoulder into a left lower level block.

23. Stepping forward with a sliding motion with the right foot into a horse-

68. Customarily there is a kiai at this point in the kata. [Translator's note.]

69. It is difficult to distinguish between "execute" and "assume the position" in this case and in Movement 19. "Execution" or "thrust" implies an attack, whereas "assume the position" implies placing the hand for protective purposes. [Translator's note.]

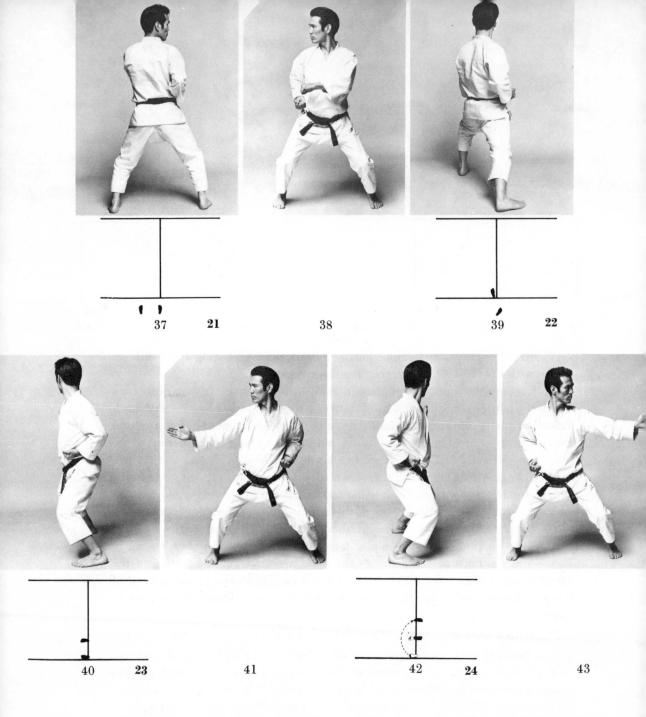

37   **21**

38

39   **22**

40   **23**

41

42   **24**

43

riding stance, swing in the right palm from the side in a middle level block; at the end of the block, the right shoulder is toward the front, and the body is in a full half-facing position. The left fist is retracted to the left hip.

24. Stepping forward in a sliding motion with the left foot into a horse-riding stance (body facing in the direction opposite to that in Movement 23), swing the left palm in from the side to execute a middle level block. At the end of the motion, the left shoulder is directed toward the front and the body is in a full half-facing position. The right fist has been retracted to the right hip. This movement is the mirror image of Movement 23.

| 44 | 25 | 45 | 46 | 26 | 47 | 27 |

25. Stepping forward with a sliding motion of the right foot into a horse-riding stance, swing the right palm inward from the side to execute a middle level block. This movement is identical to Movement 23.

26. Pivoting on the right foot, turn through 90 degrees to the left (counter-clockwise) to bring the left foot onto the left branch of Line 1 and bend the right knee slightly to assume a right back stance. At the same time, in a ripping motion of the arms, perform a right upper level block with the right fist and a lower level block with the left fist, the arms starting with the right crossed under the left and the face directed to the left.

27. Sliding the right foot to the left and straightening up with feet touching in a feet-together stance, while looking to the left, bend the left elbow to form a right angle, holding it out to the left, and place the right fist, with fingers upward, on the inner surface of the left elbow. This is the two-handed upper level block to the left side.

28. Keeping the left foot in place, slide the right foot to the right along Line 1

| 48 | 49 | 28 | 50 | 29, 30 | 51 |

52   53   54   **31**   55

into a left back stance, at the same time executing, with a ripping motion, an upper level block with the left fist and a lower level block with the right, the motion starting with the left fist below the right. The face is directed to the right.

29. Slide the left foot to the right and stand upright with the feet touching in the feet-together stance. At the same time, assume the posture of a two-handed upper level block to the right, as shown in figure 50. This movement is the mirror image of Movement 27.

30. Without moving the feet, face straight ahead and slowly lower the fists to the sides, making an opening block with the right hand inside as the fists cross on the way down.

31. Facing along Line 2, leap forward onto the right foot, drawing the left foot up behind the right heel. Land, as shown in figure 54, with the hips lowered and the wrists crossed, the right above the left, to block with the wrists against a lower level kick.

56   **32**   57   58   **33**   59

60   **34 37**   61   62   63

32. Move the left foot a step to the back, swing both fists from the crossed wrists position toward the back on either side. In this movement, the kicking foot of the opponent has been grasped with either the left or the right hand and is being pulled to that side.

33. Without moving the right foot, step forward with the left foot, and simultaneously execute a middle level opening block, the right wrist first crossing inside the left, the two then separating.

34. Stepping forward with the right foot into a front stance, raise both fists over the forehead, the right in front of the left, in an upper level scissors block, as shown in figure 60.

Note that the preceding three movements have been designed to provide an ingenious combination of techniques involving the lower, middle, and upper levels, thus allowing for a very interesting range of possibilities. Those who wish to study karate must seek such points in the kata and work to appreciate them.

64   65   66   67

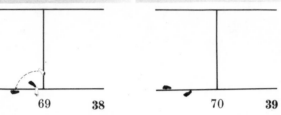

68   69   **38**   70   **39**   71

35. Without moving from the previous stance, attack the face of the opponent with a right back fist.

36. Without moving the body, simultaneously block with the left palm, covering the opponent's attack, and raise the right fist high over the right shoulder, bending the right elbow.

37. Attack directly to the front with the right back fist to the opponent's philtrum. At the end of the attack, the right elbow is resting on the upper surface of the left wrist, which has been brought up to it from below. Refer to figure 34 of Tekki Shodan. Movements 35 through 37 should be executed swiftly in a single, continous motion once they have been learned well.

38. Pivoting counterclockwise on the right foot, coming to face along the right branch of Line 3 and assuming a front stance, execute a left middle level forearm block.

39. Advance the right foot along this branch of the line of movement, simultaneously withdrawing the left fist to the hip and executing a right middle level front attack.

72   **40**   73   **41**   74   **42**

75   76   77   **43**   78

40. Pivot to the right on the left foot, coming to face in the opposite direction along Line 3, and simultaneously execute a right middle level forearm block and pull the left fist to the hip.

41. Step forward into a front stance with the left foot, simultaneously pulling the right fist to the hip and attacking with a left middle level front attack. The previous four movements, involving the same technique to the left and to the right, are executed in a similar fashion.

42. Pivoting to the left on the right foot, step onto Line 2 with the left foot into a front stance, facing along this line, while simultaneously executing a down block with the left fist and drawing the right fist to the right hip.

43. Lifting high both the right fist and foot, as shown in figure 75, stamp in strongly with the right foot, simultaneously striking down the opponent's upper level attacking arm with the right hammer block.

44. Lifting high the left fist and foot, stamp into an opponent with the left foot and block his upper level attack downward with the left wrist.

79   **44**   80   **45**   81   82   **46**

83   84   47   85   86

45. Lifting high the right fist and foot, simultaneously stamp into the opponent with the right foot and block his upper level attack with the right wrist.

46. Pivoting on the right foot, turn counterclockwise to bring the left foot onto Line 1. Simultaneously, cross the right arm over the left, with the fingers of both fists downward. Then (facing to the left), with a sliding motion to the left and a ripping motion of the hands, extend the left fist to the left and draw the right fist to a position in front of the chest as shown in figure 82.

47. In the mirror image of the preceding movement, crossing the left arm over the right, execute a sliding motion to the right, and with a ripping motion of the hands, simultaneously extend the right fist to the right and pull the left fist to a position in front of the chest.[70] The face is directed to the right. The meaning of these movements is that of grasping a fist attacking from the side and drawing it in, while at the same time attacking the opponent's side at a point below the armpit.

Yame. Slowly drawing the right foot in to the left and the hands to their starting positions, assume the yōi posture.

Such forms as Empi, Gankaku, and the present one, Jion, are fine forms, taking on ever more meaning the longer they are practiced.

TEN NO KATA OMOTE

The Ten no Kata may be called the introductory kata to sparring, and thus it is a kata for sparring to be practiced by oneself. Always imagine an opponent and practice this form diligently.

This form is composed of three sections:

    1. Parts A through D consist of the basics of the thrust.

    2. Parts E through G contain a combination of the middle level block and a thrust.

---

70. Customarily there is a kiai at this point in the kata. [Translator's note.]

3. Parts H through J contain a combination of an upper level block and a thrust.

The basics of the thrust-punch are divided first into front punch and reverse punch, and these are further divided into middle level and upper level attacks.

The stances include natural, front, back, and immovable.

The combination middle level block and thrust is used against an opponent's middle level attack by blocking and countering with a thrust. This combination is used in three of the parts.

Similarly, the combination of the upper level block and thrust is used against an opponent's upper level attack by employing an upper level block and countering with a thrust and is included three times in the form.

In practicing the block-thrust combinations, the block and the thrust should first be practiced as separate motions, as shown in the illustrations, but the principle of the combination is based on one movement. After learning the movements, they should be executed as one.

In all fist or spear hand attacks, the moment of focus (*kimete*, literally, deciding blow) should be accompanied by a vigorous kiai.

At all times, imagine an opponent before you and execute the form with full strength, keeping your eyes fixed on the imagined opponent and your mind alert to his presence.

A. Middle level front attack.

Yōi. Assume the natural stance as shown in figure 1, settling and keeping the power in the lower abdomen and standing calmly, ready to react to any circumstance.

1. Execute a right middle level front punch. The fist could, in the beginning, be drawn back to the hip before thrusting it outward, but it should be kept in mind that after the technique is learned, the thrust should start from the yōi position of the fist. The stance is front.

2. Return to the yōi position. This movement is executed slowly.

3. Execute a left front punch (see figure 3).

4. Return to the yōi position.

1   2   3

4 5

B. Upper level front punch.

1. This movement is the same as that in A1 above, except that the attack is an upper level attack.

2. This movement is similar to A2 above.

3. This movement is similar to that of B1, except that the left fist is used instead of the right, as shown in figure 5.

4. This movement is similar to A4 above.

C. Middle level reverse punch.

1. Execute a right reverse punch as shown in figure 6. While stepping forward with the left foot, thrust the right fist out in a reverse punch.

2. Return to the yōi position.

3. Execute a left middle level reverse punch.

4. Return to the yōi position.

D. Upper level reverse punch. This series is identical to that in C except that the attacks are upper level attacks (see figures 8 and 9).

6 7 8 9

10   11   12   13

E. Down block, middle level attack. From this series on (through series J), six movements are indicated in each case, although practicing a block-attack combination as a single movement reduces them to series of four.

1. Step backward with the right foot to assume a left immovable stance, at the same time executing a left down block as shown in figure 10. Imagining an attack to the lower abdomen or solar plexus level, one is blocking downward with the left fist.

2. Execute a middle level reverse punch, as shown in figure 11; after repeated practice, 1 and 2 will be executed in one movement.

3. Return to the yōi position.

4. and **5.** These are the mirror images of Movements 1 and 2, respectively.

6. Return to the yōi position.

F. Middle level forearm block, middle level reverse punch. The sequence is identical to that in E, except that the down block is changed to a middle level forearm block, as shown in figures 14 and 16.

14   15   16   17

TEN NO KATA OMOTE 205

18   19   20   21

G. Middle level sword hand block, middle level spear hand.

1. Drop the right foot back to assume a left back stance and execute a middle level sword hand block, as shown in figure 18.

2. Attack with the right spear hand as shown in figure 19, paying particular attention to the shift from back stance to immovable stance.

3. Return to the yōi position.

4. and **5.** These are the mirror images of 1 and 2, respectively.

6. Return to the yōi position.

In series H through J, the movements analogous to 4 through 6 here will be omitted from the descriptions.

H. Upper level swinging block with sword hand (shutō-barai), upper level attack.

1. Drop the right foot back and execute a left upper level sword hand block

22   23   24   25

26   27   28   29

as shown in figure 22. The intent here is to block away an opponent's upper level attack.

2. Execute a right upper level reverse punch, as shown in figure 23.

3. Return to the yōi position.

4. through **6.** Note comment in section G concerning these movements.

I. Upper level rising block, middle level reverse punch.

1. Execute a left upper level rising block as shown in figure 26. The intent here is to dodge underneath an opponent's upper level attack and block it away.

2. Execute a right middle level reverse punch.

3. Return to the yōi position.

J. Upper level iron hammer block (uchikomi), middle level attack.

1. Step backward with the right foot into an immovable stance while executing an iron hammer block with the left fist as shown in figure 30 (i.e., raising the left fist high over the head, strike downward in a semicircular motion). The

30   31   32   33

point here is to avoid an opponent's upper level attack by shifting the body into a half-facing stance while blocking the attack away.

   2. Execute a right middle level reverse punch.

   3. Return to the yōi position.

CHAPTER 5

ENGAGEMENT MATCHES

Demonstrations of kumite. From the first edition.

CHAPTER 5 ENGAGEMENT MATCHES

SIGNIFICANCE OF MATCHING

Sparring (*kumite*) is a form used to apply offensive and defensive techniques, practiced in the kata, under more realistic conditions, in which by prearrangement between participants one applies offensive and the other defensive techniques. It might be difficult for a spirited young man to understand the purpose of kata, so he will find it interesting after gaining some proficiency in the kata to practice sparring if he can find an appropriate partner and a suitable training area. However, it must be emphasized that sparring does not exist apart from the kata but for the practice of kata, so naturally there should be no corrupting influence on one's kata from sparring practice. When one becomes enthusiastic about sparring, there is a tendency for his kata to become bad. Karate, to the very end, should be practiced with kata as the principal method and sparring as a supporting method.

It has long been said that there is no first hand (sente) in Karate,[1] and whether performing kata or kumite, the front fist is used for defense and the fist held to the back is used for offense. Consequently, immediately following (without a hairbreadth delay) the blocking of an opponent's attack with the front fist, the rear fist is used to destroy the opponent. If at this moment, there is even the slightest delay in the movement, one will then be forced inescapably into the predicament of maintaining a defensive role. The Japanese phrase *go no sen o toru* means simply "defense equals offense." This should give an insight into the relationship between defense and offense. However there are times, depending upon the moment, or adjusting to a changing situation, when the defensive hand becomes an offensive hand. This is called "*hente*" ("changing hands"), and frequently in actual cases it is more effective than the orthodox use. The effective use of this technique will indicate one's technical level.

The front hand held in defense and the hand held back in the offensive position are variously contrasted as follows:

front (defensive) hand	rear (offensive) hand
death hand (*shi-te*)	life hand (*katsu-te*)
female hand (*me-te*)	male hand (*o-te*)
yang hand (*yō no te*)	yin hand (*in no te*)
regular hand (*sei no te*)	irregular hand (*ki no te*)

It has been said by our elders that "the essence of combat lies in between *sei* and *ki* [or the regular and the irregular], and without attaining the ability

---

1. The meaning is that in karate there is no advantage to the one who makes the first attack. [Translator's note.]

of changing *sei* into *ki* and *ki* into *sei* how can one attain victory?" And also, "As yin and yang have no beginning, and movement or non-movement do not appear, who can win but one who knows the *Dō* [Way]?"; thus since the essence of karate is found truly between ki and sei or between *in* (yin) and *yō* (yang), those who study karate must diligently muse upon these words.

A technique that has been called one of the secret techniques of karate is the triangle leap (*sankaku tobi*). This technique is used to escape from critical life-and-death situations such as being at the edge of a high cliff in combat and suddenly reversing the positions by leaping in a triangular manner and gaining the offensive. It is not, as commonly and mistakenly described in the streets, a technique where one leaps about indiscriminately. One will learn this technique with long training. There are the Ten no Kata Ura, triple engagement (*sambon-gumite*), single engagement (*ippon-gumite*) as basic sparring, and there is free engagement (*jiyū kumite*) for practice matches.

BASIC SPARRING

TEN NO KATA URA

Ten no Kata Ura is the first form of practice in which an opponent is involved. Up to this point an opponent was just imagined in training, but with a real opponent involved, there is some danger and at the same time more seriousness. Thus extra care in maintaining a correct posture and stopping the fist within an inch of the vital point becomes extremely important. At the beginning of the performance both parties stand facing each other with a suitable distance between them, and one must not forget to bow to the opponent with a humble spirit. This also applies at the end of the performance.

The six parts of this ura portion of the Ten no Kata consist of parts E through J of the omote portion of the kata arranged so that they may be performed together by two people.

When practicing, the partners should prearrange to alternately assume the attacking and defending parts.

Both the attacking and defending partners should exert sufficient strength

1   2

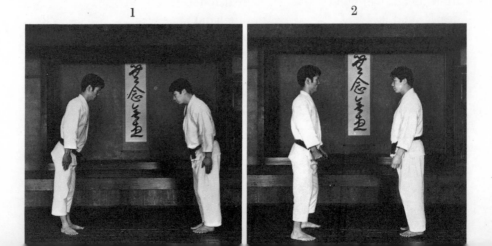

in the lower abdomen (*tanden*) and emit a kiai at the precise moment that the techniques are applied.

When performing, both attacker and defender should exert themselves with seriousness to their utmost capability.

One's intention must be to practice so that the block and attack are executed as one movement.

The distance to be maintained between the opponents should be carefully studied.

A. Down block, middle level reverse punch.

1. Attacker (*tsuki-te*): Execute a lower level or middle level front punch together with a kiai (see figure 3).

Defender (*uke-te*): Step back with the right foot and execute a down block with the left arm. This is called "inside block." When stepping back with the left foot and blocking with the right arm it is called "outside block." The photos for A through F are all shown with inside block, but the outside block should also be practiced.

2. Defender: Execute a middle level reverse punch with the right fist. After learning the techniques well, the uke movements of 1 and 2 should all be executed in one continuous movement as in the omote of Ten no Kata. At this time, the defender should not allow the attacker a chance to strike with his left fist. The movements of blocking and attacking must be one continuous movement. Also, one must figure out a way to destroy the opponent's balance. On the other hand, the attacker must remember to maintain his balance even after having the attack blocked and be ready to attack again instantly.

3. Both attacker and defender return to the yōi stance.

4, 5 and **6.** As in the omote of Ten no Kata, execute the above movements with the opposite side; then both opponents return to the yōi stance. (In the following sections, B through H, the movements for the opposite side will not be explained.)

B. Middle level inside forearm block, middle level reverse punch.

1. Attacker: Execute a right middle level front punch.

Defender: Execute a left middle level inside forearm block as shown in figure 6.

2. Defender: Execute a middle level reverse punch as shown in figure 7.

3. Return to the yōi stance.

6   7

8   9

C. Middle level sword hand block, middle level spear hand.

1. Attacker: Execute a right middle level front punch.

Defender: Step back with the right foot and with the left sword hand, block away the opponent's wrist. Assuming a back stance, be ready for a kick to the opponent's groin or solar plexus with the left foot. Refer to figure 8.

2. Defender: Extending the four fingers of the right hand, thrust at the opponent's midsection, as shown in figure 9. Shift from the back stance to the immovable stance.

3. Both return to the yōi stance.

D. Upper level sword hand block, upper level reverse punch.

1. Attacker: Execute a right upper level front punch.

10   11

Defender: Step back with the right foot, and with the left sword hand knock away the opponent's wrist or forearm. Refer to figure 10.

2. Defender: Execute a right upper level reverse punch, or grasp the opponent's wrist and execute an upper level reverse punch while pulling in the opponent.

3. Both return to the yōi stance.

12   13

E. Upper level rising block, middle level reverse punch.

1. Attacker: Execute a right upper level front punch.

Defender: Lowering the hips and stepping back with the right foot, execute an upper level rising block with the left arm. The intention here is to hit the opponent's chin or armpit. Refer to figure 12.

2. Defender: Execute a middle level reverse punch with the right fist. Refer to figure 13.

3. Both return to the yōi stance.

F. Upper level iron hammer block, middle level reverse punch.

1. Attacker: Execute a right upper level front punch.

Defender: Step back with the left foot and raising the right fist hit the opponent's arm with the wrist. The feeling here is to hit the opponent's face with the raised right fist, follow through with a block to the opponent's

14   15

arm, and attack the opponent's solar plexus with the elbow at the same time. Refer to figure 14.

2. Defender: Execute a middle level reverse punch with the left fist. Refer to figure 15.

3. Both return to the yōi stance.

TRIPLE ENGAGEMENT MATCH (SAMBON-GUMITE)

As mentioned in the Ten no Kata, the opponents bow to each other after assuming positions with an appropriate distance between them. Following this, at the command of yōi the attacker takes a step back with his right foot to assume the down block posture while the defender keeps his natural stance, as shown in figure 3. At this time, the attacker must thrust in with the intention of not allowing his opponent any opportunity to block his thrust, and at the same time it is important for the defender to be prepared to react appropriately to any attack; attention should not be distracted by concern for the correctness of the form.

1   2

3   4   5

6   7   8

At the ensuing counts of one, two and three the attacker advances thrusting to the upper, middle, or lower level in whatever order has been agreed upon before the beginning of the triple engagement. The defender will step back, practicing blocks such as upper level rising block, down block and so on, and at the same time as the last block at the count of three, he will also attack the opponent's vital points such as the philtrum, solar plexus and so on for the decisive blow. At the command of either "Yame" or "Naore," the attacker will withdraw his forward foot, and the defender will bring up his rear foot, both assuming the natural stance and face each other, and until the command of "Yasume" ("rest") is given, the opponents must not shift their eyes or move their limbs needlessly. This is called keeping the "mind in reserve,"

9   10   11

12   13   14

15   16

17   18

that is; preserving one's alertness (literally, "remaining mind," or *zanshin*).

Triple engagment is practiced in this manner in a series of three alternating movements: right, left, right, one side then the other. Next the defender switches to become the attacker and vice-versa, and practice continues. The beginner will practice the attacker's and defender's techniques, keeping in time with the counts of one, two and three; it is important at this time to maintain the correct position of the hips and legs, and to correct the overall posture, but as one gradually improves, practice of *oikomi* should begin. In other words, instead of keeping time to the count of one, two and three, the attacker should deliver

19   20

21   22

his series of thrusts swiftly to keep the initiative, even as the opponent is himself trying to take away the initiative. Thus the attacker practices overwhelming the defender by not allowing him any chance of recovery; whereas the defender must practice to perfect the control of his body so as to move away from the attacks, trying to discover for himself the secret art of escaping from the brink of death by a hairbreadth.

SINGLE ENGAGEMENT MATCH (IPPON-GUMITE)

After bowing to each other, the opponents swiftly separate, taking up positions at an appropriate distance, as shown in figure 3; the attacker will adjust his breathing rhythm and distance and attack the opponent in the area agreed on before the match. It may be the upper, middle or lower level, or it may be a kicking attack. (Kicking techniques are explained in detail in chapter 2.) The defender will move accordingly to the front, back or either side, using blocking techniques and swiftly executing a decisive technique. At this time, the attacker should be experimenting with methods to make ineffective the defender's decisive blow and returning a decisive technique of

1   2   3

4   5   6

his own. Differing from the triple engagement, the decisive blow is accomplished after a single attack. The accurate measurement of the appropriate distance (*ma*) is very important at this time.

KICKING MATCHES

Kicking techniques have been considered a specialty of karate, but actually they are less orthodox than hand techniques. Furthermore one cannot forget that at the moment of kicking one will be in the precarious position of standing on one leg, so kicks should be practiced with this thought in mind.

1   2

Kicking techniques against fist thrusts (tsuki). When the opponent attacks with a right fist thrust to the upper section, this attack is warded away with an upper level rising block and followed up with a front kick to the opponent's groin with the right foot. Of course the left foot may be used for this attack also. Depending upon one's distance from the opponent, one may advance or retreat to kick. Refer to figure 1.

When the opponent attacks with a right fist thrust to the midsection, one shifts to a half-facing stance and attacks the opponent with a roundhouse kick, aiming for the groin or solar plexus. Refer to figure 2.

When the opponent attacks the upper section with a right fist thrust, kick into the opponent's side with a side thrust kick (yoko-geri), timing the attack to coincide with the start of the opponent's attack. Refer to figure 3.

3   4

When the opponent attacks with a right fist thrust to the upper section, lower the body slightly and, using a side-up kick with the right foot, kick the opponent's arm pit (*waki kage*, a vital point). Refer to figure 4.

Blocking techniques against kicks. When the opponent attacks with a front kick with the right foot, assume a half-facing stance to the right, and blocking the kick with the left fist, attack the opponent's face or solar plexus with the right fist. Refer to figures 5 and 6.

When the opponent attacks with a side thrust kick to the chest or solar plexus with his right foot, assume a right half-facing stance, and kick the opponent's testicles with a front kick, using the right foot. Refer to figures 7 and 8.

When the opponent attacks with a side-up kick (yoko-geri keage), leaping in and kicking with his right foot, assume a left half-facing stance, and at the same time strike at the opponent's testicles with a left fist thrust or a front kick with the right foot. Refer to figures 7 and 8.

5   6

7

8

9

10

When the opponent attacks with a right foot roundhouse kick (mawashigeri) to the side, chest or solar plexus, step back a half step assuming a left half-facing position, and avoiding the kick, quickly utilize the advantage to step in and attack the opponent's side with a left fist thrust. Refer to figure 9. Or jump with the start of the opponent's kick, and attack the opponent's solar plexus with a right fist thrust. Refer to figure 10.

Since the above explanations are concerned only with the basics of sparring, one should experiment with and practice other sparring techniques and also practice a series of different types of attacks and blocks.

FREE SPARRING

Until now practice has called for prior designation of attacker and defender, as well as agreement beforehand on the type of attack, limiting it to fist attacks to the upper, middle and lower levels plus kicking attacks. But in free sparring (*jiyū kumite*), there are no set rules as to who will be the attacker or defender, and so either one may freely attack, but there is one agreement: the attacks will be stopped short of the vital points, leaving a thin margin.

1   2   3

At this time, without long and repeated practice, one can easily injure the opponent inadvertently, so one must repeatedly remind himself to be very careful about his ability to control his attacks before engaging in free sparring. Beginning students must refrain at all times from heedlessly engaging in free sparring. If one has picked the appropriate distance and the moment in rhythm, the deciding technique can be delivered, and, if it were a real combat situation, the contest would be ended, so no pushing or grappling is allowed. Frequently one sees matches that resemble cockfights, but people engaging in such matches should be considered as among those who do not really understand what a free engagement match is; thus they will not be able to even faintly discern the highly skilled level of an attack that never misses the vital point and that could be considered as the essence of karate technique. It is hoped that the chapter on the trainee's maxims will be thoroughly studied and understood.

Furthermore, the matching up to the single engagement match was a process of learning defensive and offensive techniques, but in free engagement, the restrictions of action have been lifted as mentioned above, and it may be compared to an actual duel as in other martial arts where all possible defensive and offensive techniques can be fully used. It is important to keep this in mind and really understand the exquisite mystery inherent in free engagement.

IAI

Sparring which begins with both the offensive and defensive opponents seated and facing each other is called *iai*. Thus it is only the application of basic techniques as in the other engagement forms so far explained. Therefore the basic forms and sparring forms learned should be applied and studied by each individual. If the engagement were to be divided, it could be split into two situations: attack coming from the front and attack coming from the back. These in turn may be separated into attacks grasping one wrist, grasping both wrists, strangling, and so on, and by imagining all types of attacks one will be able to devise innumerable variations of counterattacks.[2]

---

2. Explanations and demonstrations have been added by the translator to supplement the original text.

1   2

3   4

*A***1.** Defender and attacker sit facing each other. They bow.

2. The attacker moves toward the defender with the right leg, grasping the defender's left wrist with the right hand, as shown in figure 3.

3. The defender turns to his left, sliding the left knee as the hips and body turn, breaking the attacker's balance. At the same time, the defender draws his right arm to his left shoulder.

4. The defender strikes with the right sword hand to the attacker's right temple, or neck.

*B***1.** From a sitting position, the attacker advances the right leg, grasping the

5   6

defender's right wrist with the left hand and the right arm with the right hand.

2. The defender rotates his right wrist clockwise over the attacker's two arms and raises the right knee, breaking the attacker's balance.

3. The defender immediately follows with a left fist attack to the attacker's face. Refer to figure 6.

7   8

*C***1.** From a sitting position, the attacker moves toward the defender with the right leg and executes a right front punch to the face.

2. The defender blocks the punch with a right rising block.

3. The defender catches the attacker's right wrist with his right hand and draws the arm to his own right hip, simultaneously pivoting on the right knee and raising the left leg. Refer to figure 8.

4. The defender punches the right side of the attacker's body with the left fist.

*D***1.** From a sitting position, the attacker advances his right leg and executes a right front punch to the face, as in C1. Refer to figure 9.

2. The defender blocks the punch with a left rising block.

3. The defender catches the attacker's right wrist with the left hand and

9   10

draws the arm to his own left hip, simultaneously pivoting and raising the right leg.

4. The defender immediately follows with a right fist attack to the attacker's face.

11   12   13

E1. The attacker encircles the seated defender from behind, pinning the defender's arms to his sides, as shown in figure 11.

2. Raising the right arm and right leg, the defender breaks the attacker's hold, driving his left elbow to the attacker's solar plexus.

3. The defender follows with a left sword hand attack to the attacker's groin.

F1. From a sitting position, the attacker moves toward the defender with the right leg and executes a right front punch to the face.

2. The defender avoids the punch by falling to his left, supports his upper body with the palms of his hands on the floor, and delivers a roundhouse kick to the attacker's solar plexus. Refer to figure 14.

G1. From a sitting position, the attacker moves toward the defender with the right leg and executes a right front punch to the face.

14   15

2. The defender escapes the punch by falling backward and slightly to the left, supports his upper body with the palms of both hands flat on the floor, and delivers a side-thrust kick to the midsection. Refer to figure 15.

THROWING TECHNIQUES

Karate may be said to be hard technique when compared to the soft technique of jujitsu, but softness includes hardness and hardness includes softness. In other words, softness is necessary to become hard, and hardness is necessary to become soft, and to begin with, both softness and hardness are one.

Thus in karate, hitting, thrusting, and kicking are not the only methods; throwing techniques (*nagewaza*) and pressure against joints are also included. Depending upon the strength and skill of the opponent it is not always necessary to use powerful techniques like hitting, thrusting, and kicking, but, adjusting to the situation, softer techniques such as throwing may be used, and in this versatility there is an inexpressible savor. Whether throwing techniques or joint-pressure techniques, there are, as stated previously in the explanation of sparring and iai, innumerable techniques, and the important thing is to adjust according to the opponent, so the use of these techniques will be left to the discretion of the researcher. One must always keep in mind that since the essence of karate is found in a single thrust or kick, and one should never be grasped by or grapple with an opponent, one must be very careful not to be defeated through concern with throwing an opponent or applying a joint-punishment hold.

Throwing techniques include *byōbudaoshi, komanage, kubiwa, katawaguruma, tsubamegaeshi, yaridama, taniotoshi, udewa, sakatsuchi,* and others.[3] All these techniques should be studied, referring to basic kata.

1   2   3

3. Explanations and demonstrations have been added by the translator to supplement the original text.

Byōbudaoshi (To topple a folding screen)

1. The opponent attacks the upper level from a down block posture.

2. Block with the left open hand as you step back with the right leg.

3. Simultaneously step behind the opponent's right leg with the right leg, attack the opponent's chin with the right palm, and sweep the opponent's leg.

4   5

Komanage (Spinning top)

1. The opponent attacks the upper level from a down block posture.

2. Simultaneously step back with the left leg and block the opponent's hand with the right wrist. Refer to figure 4.

3. Grasp the opponent's right wrist while placing the left hand in his armpit, simultaneously stepping forward with the left foot.

4. Force the opponent's arm down and to his right while pivoting to the right on the left foot.

6   7

8   9

Kubiwa (To encircle the neck)

1. The opponent attacks the upper level from a down block posture.

2. Step back with the left foot and block the opponent's upper level attack with the right wrist, hooking the opponent's arm down and to the right.

3. Slide the right foot forward and simultaneously attack the opponent's chin, as shown in figure 8.

4. While continuing to slide the right leg forward encircle the opponent's neck with the right arm. Force the opponent's head and upper body over backward, throwing the opponent to the ground.

Katawaguruma (Half wheel)

1. The opponent attacks the upper level from a down block posture.

2. Block the opponent's middle level attack by hooking downwards with the right wrist while stepping back with the left leg.

3. Slide the right leg forward, inside the opponent's right leg, while grasping the opponent's neck with the right arm, and place your left hand under the opponent's right thigh.

4. Lift the opponent's right leg up and pull his neck over to the right, lifting and throwing him. Refer to figure 12.

10   11   12

13   14

15   16

Tsubamegaeshi (V-turning swallow)

   1. The opponent attacks the upper level from a down block posture.

   2. Step back with the left leg while executing an upper level scissors block.

   3. Grasp the opponent's right wrist with the left hand and pull him in while attacking his face with a right back punch, as shown in figure 14.

   4. Hold the opponent's elbow with the right hand, pivot counterclockwise on the right leg, lowering the body and kneeling on the left knee, and pull the opponent's arm to throw him.

Yaridama (To spear a ball)

   1. The opponent attacks the upper level from a down block posture.

17   18

2. Step in with the right leg while blocking the opponent's upper level attack with the left hand and placing the right hand in the opponent's crotch.

3. Pull the opponent's right arm forward while lifting him up and throw him.

19

20

21

22

Taniotoshi (To push off a cliff)

1. The opponent attacks the upper level from a down block posture.

2. Step back with the left leg, simultaneously blocking the opponent's attack with the left hand and striking his solar plexus with the right fist.

3. Step across the opponent's right leg with the right leg while grasping his upper arm with the right arm. Refer to figure 20.

4. Throw the opponent down with the motion of the hips.

Udewa (To encircle with the arm)

1. The opponent attacks with a two-hand attack.

2. Stepping back with the left leg, execute a two-hand upper level rising block. Refer to figure 23.

23   24   25

3. Sliding forward with the right foot, execute a two-fist hammer attack to the opponent's sides.

4. Sliding in deeper, tackle opponent.

Sakatsuchi (To hammer upside down)

1. The opponent attacks the upper level with a right front punch.

2. Step back with the left leg while executing an upper level rising block with the right arm.

3. Slide the right shoulder under the opponent's armpit while sliding forward with the right leg, dropping the hips and placing the left hand in back of the opponent's left thigh, as shown in figure 27.

4. Lift and overturn the opponent, and drive his head into the ground.

26

27

28

29

WEAPONS AND KARATE-DŌ

In karate from the beginning, the bare hands and feet have been considered as blades, and it should be practiced with the idea that they will cut when touched, so there is no need to be especially cautious when faced with a weapon, but it goes without saying that distance and body shifting methods should be varied depending on the type of weapon that is used by the opponent.

When sufficient skill has been acquired through practice, a sword, dagger, stick and so on should actually be used in practice to learn the techniques against these weapons and to prepare oneself mentally against them.

On the other hand, when one is using a weapon, it is natural to begin depending upon it and consequently lose readiness in the use of the feet, the elbows and the free hand. Should an opponent neutralize the weapon, one could become weaker than a weaponless man.

When actually faced with a weapon, one's coat and shoes are useful, and even a handkerchief or piece of paper could become effective defensive weapons, depending upon their use. One could spit upon the opponent's face, emit a kiai, stamp one's foot or clap one's hands to distract the opponent as other means of defensive actions. Therefore, keeping in mind these methods, one will be able to easily control an opponent with a weapon.

SELF-DEFENSE FOR WOMEN

Women's self-defense somehow gives the impression of hardness and masculinity, and unfortunately this tends to create the misunderstanding among the public that the practice of karate will lead to ungracefulness, which is not at all the case. A sound mind in a sound body is a saying that applies not only to men but also to women. This saying may be changed to, "A sound child in a sound mother." It may be clearer to say that women's self-defense includes physical culture and calisthenics as well as self-defense. Health is not limited to a sound body, but rather that must be combined with a healthy mind. Further you may agree that the objective of karate is to instill the spirit of humbleness or modesty. There should not be any objection to training that will develop a healthy mind, a healthy body, and a gentle spirit that at the same time knows the arts of self-defense. This section should be read with the above thoughts in mind.

OBJECTIVES

The objective of martial arts has always been to defend oneself and not to attack others, and in the case of women's self-defense this is especially true. If the physically delicate woman contests the attacks of a ruffian with physical force it is almost impossible for her to defend herself. Thus as noted earlier, when attacked, it is possible to easily escape from danger through knowledge of self-defense; so by all means the fundamentals of self-defense should be ready for application at all times. The comparative weakness of a woman in protecting herself from a more powerful opponent must be offset by her quick and especially accurate techniques in attacking the vital points. In order to achieve this, one must practice regularly; otherwise, during emergencies, one might hesitate or become excited and increase the danger instead of avoiding it. One should first practice forms and basic techniques and eventually work up to sparring practice as one becomes more skillful, imagining situations that women encounter most and constantly practicing them so that in a dangerous situation one may escape without harm. Training also is an excellent form of healthful exercise, and may cultivate overall physical beauty for women who are prone to lead sedentary lives.

SECRET PRINCIPLES

Crude tactics are a source of serious injuries (a little learning is a dangerous thing) is a proverb often quoted, and similarly, with just a little knowledge of the martial arts, one might become careless and adversely incur injuries with lifelong consequences, so one must always remember to be very careful.

The secret principle of martial arts is not vanquishing the attacker but resolving to avoid an encounter before its occurrence. To become the object of an attack is an indication that there was an opening in one's guard, and the important thing is to be on guard at all times. One should refrain from walking alone at night as much as possible, and when that is unavoidable, one should take a roundabout route to avoid dangerous neighborhoods.

If, even while taking precautionary measures, one should be attacked by hoodlums in a stroke of ill luck, then it is better to run away. Running away as far as possible and seeking shelter in someone's home or shouting for help would be the best forms of self-defense. Many times out of shyness women will not seek shelter in another's home or seek other help even when in danger of bodily harm. But to be so timid at times like these would be playing right into the hands of the attackers.

When there are no avenues of escape or one is caught even before any attempt to escape can be made, then for the first time the use of self-defense techniques should be considered. Even at times like these, do not show any intention of attacking, but first let the attacker become careless. At that time attack him, concentrating one's whole strength in one blow to a vital point, and in the moment of surprise, escape and seek shelter or help. It is most important to be on guard without becoming excited and to act with presence of mind throughout such a situation from the beginning and even once the situation is in hand.

When delivering the one blow against the attacker, the importance of using one's whole strength and being especially accurate cannot be overemphasized. In the event that this one blow is ineffective, the attacker will become more violent, a point not to be forgotten. The importance of using one's whole strength and putting one's heart and soul in this one attempt has been stressed, but it is also important to do so only after reaching a rational conclusion that there is no other way out.

METHODS OF PRACTICE

The methods of practicing self-defense should be in accordance with chapter 4, part 2, "Advice on Training." Chapter 2, Fundamental Elements, should be studied regarding kicking and thrusting techniques. When practicing, one should imagine various situations, especially sparring, *iai* and escape techniques (*tori-te*). The attacker may grasp the wrists, clothing, neck, or other parts of the body, and one must escape from his attempt to grasp and immediately deliver a counterattack. So the point to remember is the quickness of the counterattack, which is executed almost simultaneously while escaping from the attacker's hold. The techniques for escaping and counterattacking must be analyzed and practiced separately at first, but one must try gradually to reach a point where the blocking and attacking can be executed simultaneously.

Escape techniques may be used against front, side, and rear grasping attacks. Attacks from the front may include such techniques as grasping a wrist, both wrists, the collar, hair or hugging, etc., and side attacks such as grasping the wrist and grasping the neck; also attacks from the rear may consist of similar techniques such as grasping the wrist, grasping the collar, hugging, etc. There may be times when several attackers may attack from both sides or from front and back. Considering all situations, always think about and practice against such attacks.

VITAL POINTS OF
THE HUMAN BODY

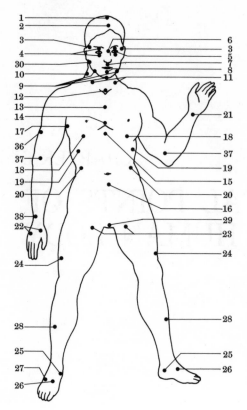
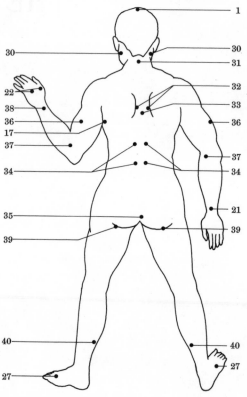

Vital Points of the Human Body (See pages 240–244 for explanation of the numbered points.)

CHAPTER 6 VITAL POINTS OF THE HUMAN BODY

DEFINITION

It is advantageous to those who train in Karate-dō to know about the vital points (*jintai kyūsho*) of the human body. For example, if the face is attacked with equal strength first at a random point and next at a vital point, there would be a considerable difference in the effect of the blows. In other words, by vital points, the parts of the body where a blow would be comparatively effective are specified. Vital points are vital points, and the majority of those points of the body where moxa cautery is applied [in the orient] are vital points known since ancient times. In other words, points of the body where shock to the nerves can most readily be given are all vital points. Generally speaking, the vital points of karate and judo from ancient times and the points of moxa cautery have been the same, although moxa cautery points, which are located in places difficult to attack, or points which are relatively ineffective, are not included in the vital points of karate or judo. Since the objectives of moxa cautery differ from those of karate or judo, the existence of some differences is only natural. However, in the case of karate, there are several vital points that are not considered vital points in moxa cautery or judo. Thrusting with the fingers to the eyes, kicking up with the foot to the lower part of the opponent's chin, or striking the lower part of the chin with the fist (done frequently in boxing) are some good examples of points considered vital in karate but not considered so in moxa cautery or judo.

The following section, which explains the vital points in more detail, is divided into "Causes of Death" and "Causes of Losing Consciousness." However, they are not in actuality clearcut classifications. Ideally, a division of the vital points would be into those that if struck with sufficient force would cause death and those where a similar blow may cause only loss of consciousness; in fact even those points considered to be death-causing points, such as the solar plexus, may cause only unconsciousness or not even that if struck with insufficient force. Also, areas that are not generally considered to be death-causing, such as the chest and abdomen, cannot be considered as entirely non-death-causing, for if these points are struck by a very well-trained fist, the blow may cause death through internal hemorrhage. In short, a vital point is only a point where a blow is comparatively effective.

The effectiveness of a blow is not solely due to the power of the blow itself; effectiveness will vary according to the condition of the person at the moment he is struck and how well he is trained. If a person is well trained, he will be able to withstand a blow that ordinarily would be considered a deathblow. Consider the well trained chest of a wrestler. The powerful chest developed through constant training probably will not be affected much by an amateur's punch.

My teacher, Master Itosu, had a body that could be likened to a cast-iron torso. There were many occasions at parties when everyone enjoyed a few drinks and some of the younger members would punch at the teacher, but the master smiled and kept taking sips of the wine without any indication that he even noticed the blows. The human body can be developed with training into such a powerful body as that of Master Itosu, so those who train in karate should develop, together with the training of the arms and legs for powerful strikes, literally ironlike or rocklike bodies through ceaseless effort.

THE VITAL POINTS

The most widely used names for the vital points have been used, and those points that did not already have names were given names for convenience. Since actual tests cannot be made in the classification of points into Cause of Death and Cause of Unconsciousness, knowledge transmitted through written notes and knowledge transmitted by word of mouth from the past have been used as the source. The following classification is considered to have more credibility than similar classifications that have been published so far. (Numbers in parentheses correspond to those in figures 1 and 2, page 238.)

FRONT: HEAD AND FACE

Suture, coronal (tendō): line of juncture of the frontal bone and the parietal bones. Cause of death is severe trauma to the cerebrum and disruptive stimulation of cranial nerves.(1)

Frontal fontanel (tentō): the region of the head between the forehead and the coronal suture that is exposed and seen to pulsate in a newborn infant. Cause of death is concussion and trauma to cranial nerves.(2)

Temple (kasumi): especially suture of cheek bone and frontal bone. Loss of consciousness is due to trauma to cranial nerves resulting in loss of sensory and motor function.(3)

Circumorbital region (seidon): upper and lower parts of eye socket. Loss of consciousness results from cerebral trauma and resulting loss of nervous control. (4)

Eyeball (gansei). Loss of consciousness produced by severe trauma to cerebrum resulting in disruptive stimulation of cranial nerves and loss of sensory and motor function. (5)

Glabella (uto): the point at the base of the nose between the eyes. Loss of consciousness results from severe trauma to cerebrum leading to disruptive stimulation of cranial nerves and loss of sensory and motor function. (6)

Suture, intermaxillary (jinchū): juncture of left and right upper jawbones below nose. Loss of consciousness results from trauma to cranial nerves and loss of sensory and motor function.(7)

Lower jaw, center (gekon): one-half inch below lower lip. Loss of consciousness results from trauma to cranial nerves and loss of sensory and motor function. (8)

Mandible, base (mikazuki): lower ridge of lower jaw; also the articulation below and in front of the ears. Loss of consciousness results from concussion and loss of nervous coordination. (9) (This is a vital point in karate, although it is not so considered by some schools of judo.)

A blow to any of the vital points of the face causes trauma to the cranial nerves resulting in loss of nervous coordination and consciousness as well as vascular shock. There are twelve cranial nerves, possessing sensory, motor or mixed function, as follows: olfactorius, opticus, oculomotoris, trochlearis, trigeminus, abducens, facialis, acousticus, glossopharyngeus, vagus, spinal accessorius, and hypoglossus.

FRONT: MIDDLE SECTION

Neck, side (matsukaze): the length of the sternocleidomastoid muscle covered by the platysma. Cause of loss of consciousness is trauma to the carotid artery and the pneumogastric nerve leading to shock and to loss of sensory and motor function.(10)

Supraclavicular fossa (murasame): front portion of the throat on either side, just above the collar bone at the origin of the lateral head of the sternocleidomastoid muscle. Cause of loss of consciousness is trauma to the artery located below the collar bone and to the sublingual nerve, producing shock and loss of motor function.(11)

Suprasternal notch (hichū): the concavity on the ventral surface of the neck between the sternum below and the hyoid bone above. Cause of loss of consciousness is blocking of the windpipe.(12)

Sternal angle (tanchū): just below the juncture of the manubrium and the sternum. Cause of loss of consciousness is trauma to the heart, bronchus, arteries supplying the upper part of the body, and the pulmonary artery, leading to malfunction of the respiratory system and shock.(13)

Xiphoid process (kyōsen): lowest part of the sternum. Cause of loss of consciousness is severe trauma to the liver, stomach and heart, leading to shock and to disturbance of the nervous system followed by loss of motor function. (14)

Solar plexus (suigetsu): concavity just below the sternum. Loss of consciousness is caused by trauma to the stomach and liver, leading to damage to adjacent regions above and below and in turn to effects on the nerves that produce loss of function of internal organs.(15)

Point about one inch below the umbilicus (myōjō, tanden). Loss of consciousness is caused by trauma to the small intestine and bladder and in turn to the large blood vessels and nerves in the abdomen, producing shock and loss of motor function.(16)

Subaxillary region (kyōei): fourth intercostal space. Loss of consciousness results from severe trauma to the lungs and associated nerves, leading to loss of lung function and stoppage of breathing and circulatory failure.(17)

Region below the nipples (ganka): between the fifth and sixth ribs on either side. Cause of loss of consciousness is similar to that in the preceding case, i.e., loss of lung function, stoppage of breath and circulatory failure.(18)

Abdomen, hypochondriac region (denkō): seventh intercostal space. Cause of loss of consciousness is different for the left and right sides. On the right side, it is severe trauma to the liver, leading to loss of nervous function associated with the liver and lungs. On the left side, it is severe trauma to the stomach and spleen with effects on the heart and lungs, producing loss of nervous function associated with the heart and lungs.(19)

Abdomen, lumbar region (inazuma): eleventh intercostal space. Cause of loss of consciousness is different for the left and right sides and is nearly the same as that for the hypochondriac region.(20)

Attacks to the vital points mentioned up to this point, which are located in the chest and abdominal regions, all result in primary trauma to internal organs with disruptive effects on the spinal cord and sympathetic nervous system. This in turn affects cranial nerves, leading to loss of consciousness caused by shock and by loss of sensory and motor function and consequent stoppage of breathing. It is noteworthy in this connection that attacks to vital points located in the head do not always lead to loss of breathing in spite of loss of sensory and motor function.

Wrist, inside (uchi shakutaku): between brachioradialis and flexor muscles of the fingers. An attack to this point produces trauma to the underlying nerve and artery, leading to an unusual type of pain affecting the chest and throat regions and causing loss of motor function and loss of consciousness. (21)

Hand, back (shukō): especially points between thumb and index finger and between middle and ring fingers. Cause of loss of consciousness is shock to the median nerve leading to an unusual type of pain in the chest and throat regions that produces loss of motor function. A similar result is to be expected from striking any one of the bones located at the back of the hand. (22)

FRONT: LOWER SECTION

Inguinal region (yakō): inner region of the upper thigh; part of the musculature of the pubic bones. Cause of loss of consciousness is trauma to the underlying artery and nerve, as well as to the closing nerve, causing an unusual type of pain in the hip and abdomen that produces loss of motor function.(23)

Thigh, lower, lateral part (fukuto): middle part of lateral vastus muscle. Cause of loss of consciousness is cramping of the muscle in the thigh leading to pain in the lower abdomen and loss of motor function in the leg.(24)

Medial malleolus (naike, uchikurubushi, uchikurobushi): the point just below the medial tuberosity of the tibia. Although this term usually indicates the lowest part of the shinbone, i.e., the inside surface of the ankle, *uchikurobushi* as used to identify a point of attack denotes a point on the medial surface of the tarsal bone just below the ankle. Cause of loss of consciousness is trauma to the tibial artery, causing an unusual type of pain in the hip area that leads to loss of motor function.(25)

Instep (kōri): medial portion of top of the foot. The point of attack is slightly to the inside of the medial line between the tendons of the big toe and the second toe. Cause of loss of consciousness is trauma to the nerve located in the inside portion of the sole, the tibial artery and the deep fibular nerve, causing an unusual type of pain in the leg, hip and abdomen and leading to loss of motor function.(26)

Foot, top, lateral part (sōin, kusagakure): just below the heads of the fourth and fifth metatarsals. Cause of loss of consciousness is similar to that in the preceding case.(27)

Fibula, middle (kōkotsu, mukōzune). An attack to this point produces trauma to the fibular nerve, leading to severe pain and loss of upright posture.(28)

Testes (kinteki). Cause of loss of consciousness is trauma to the nerves and arteries of the testicles and groin, inducing the testicles to rise and in turn producing loss of motor function and inability to breathe.(29)

BACK: UPPER SECTION

Concavity behind the ear (dokko): between the mastoid process and the lower jaw. Cause of loss of consciousness is trauma to cranial nerves and spinal cord, resulting in loss of sensory and motor function.(30)

Neck, back (keichū): third intervertebral space. Cause of loss of consciousness is severe trauma to cerebrum, cranial nerves and spinal cord, producing loss of sensory and motor function.(31)

BACK: MIDDLE SECTION

Scapular ridge, middle (hayauchi): the level of the third intercostal space. Cause of loss of consciousness is severe trauma to lungs and spinal cord, producing difficulty in breathing and blood circulation combined with loss of motor function.(32)

Space between fifth and sixth thoracic vertebrae (kassatsu). Cause of loss of consciousness is trauma to the spinal cord, aorta, heart and lungs, leading to loss of sensory and motor function and in turn to stoppage of breathing.(33)

Lumbar region (ushiro denkō): left and right sides of ninth and eleventh thoracic vertebrae. The two sides of the ninth thoracic vertebra are generally designated *shakkatsu denkō*, and it is said that pressing on these two points with the thumbs can relax a spasm. However, the two sides of the eleventh thoracic vertebra are more effective points for attack. Cause of loss of consciousness is severe trauma to the kidneys and associated nerve and blood vessels leading in turn to shock and loss of motor function.(34)

Spine, tip (*bitei*). Cause of loss of consciousness is trauma to the entire spinal cord, leading to cerebral trauma and loss of sensory and motor function. (35)

Upper arm, dorsal surface (*wanjun*): middle part between biceps and triceps. Cause of loss of consciousness is trauma to ulnar and median nerves and blood vessels of upper arm, producing an unsual type or pain in the chest and neck and loss of motor function.(36)

Elbow, lateral surface (*chūkitsu, hijizume*). Cause of loss of consciousness is trauma to the ulnar nerve producing an unusual type of pain in the chest and neck with loss of motor function.(37)

Wrist, dorsal surface (*sotoshakutaku*): space between ends of radius and ulna. Cause of loss of consciousness is trauma to the median nerve and loss of motor function.(38)

BACK: LOWER SECTION

Gluteal fold (*ushiro inazuma*): central portion of the back of the upper thigh just below the buttock. Cause of loss of consciousness is trauma to the sciatic nerve producing an unusual type of pain in the abdomen and hip regions and loss of motor function.(39)

Soleus muscle, lower part (*kusanagi*). Cause of loss of consciousness is trauma to tibial artery and tibial nerve, producing an unusual type of pain in the abdominal and hip regions leading in turn to loss of motor function.(40)

MAXIMS FOR THE TRAINEE

Kōmoku-ten, the guardian of the west of the four
Guardian Kings, symbolizes the *un* of *A-un*. His
expression is that of the spirit of power in reserve.
Statue in dry clay. National Treasure. Tōdai-ji
temple.

CHAPTER 7 MAXIMS FOR THE TRAINEE

The word *"bu"* of *budō* (martial arts) is written with the Chinese character for "stop" within a character signifying two crossed halberds meaning to stop conflict. Since karate is a budō, this meaning should be deeply considered, and the fists should not be used heedlessly.

Youth is justice and vigor. Vigor is stimulated by bu (martial arts) and it overflows into good or sometimes bad actions. Thus if Karate-dō is followed correctly, it will polish the character, and one will uphold justice, but if used for evil purposes, it will corrupt society and be contrary to humanity.

Force is used as a last resort where humanity and justice cannot prevail, but if the fist is used freely without consideration, then the user will lose the respect of others and be shabbily treated, while being censured for barbaric action. At any rate, the high-spirited youth in the prime of life is prone to rash speech and action, so prudence is essential.

One must have dignity without ferocity. Martial arts must bring one to this height. It will not do to act recklessly to no purpose and cause trouble for others. Masters and saints may appear as simpletons. Those who are pretentious declare to the world that they are just novice scholars or martial artists.

To stand still is to regress; those who think that they have learned everything and become conceited braggarts proclaiming their own merits after learning the movements of some kata and acquiring dexterity in their physical movements are not fit to be considered as serious trainees in the martial arts.

It is said that even a worm that is an inch long has a soul half an inch long; thus as one continues to gain skill in karate, one must become more careful with one's speech. Again, it is said that the higher the tree, the stronger the wind, but does not even the willow manage to withstand the wind? Similarly the trainee of Karate-dō must consider good behavior and humbleness as the highest of virtues.

Mencius said, "When Heaven is about to confer an important office upon a man, it first embitters his heart in its purpose; it causes him to exert his bones and sinews; it makes his body suffer hunger; it inflicts upon him want and poverty and confounds his undertakings. In this way it stimulates his will, steels his nature and thus makes him capable of accomplishing what he would otherwise be incapable of accomplishing."

If introspection reveals the self to be unjust, then no matter how base the opponent may be, will I not be afraid? If introspection reveals the self to be just, then I will go even though against a thousand or ten thousand men.

A gentleman should be gentle and never be menacing; close, yet never forward; slay but never humiliate; no sign of indecency is found in his abode; his nourishment is never heavy; even a minor mistake is corrected but there is no accusation. Thus is his strength of will.

A gentleman must be broad-minded and strong willed. The responsibilities will be heavy, and the way is long. Make benevolence your lifelong duty. This surely is an important mission. It is a lifelong effort, truly a long journey.

An ordinary man will draw his sword when ridiculed and will fight risking his life, but he may not be called a courageous man. A truly great man is not disturbed even when suddenly confronted with an unexpected event or crisis, nor angered upon finding himself in situations not of his own making, and this is because he has a great heart and his aim is high.

Eight important phrases of karate:

The mind is the same with heaven and earth.

The circulatory rhythm of the body is similar to the sun and the moon.

The Law includes hardness and softness.

Act in accordance with time and change.

Techniques will occur when a void is found.

The *Ma* requires advancing and retreating, separating and meeting.

The eyes do not miss even the slightest change.

The ears listen well in all directions.

Therefore I say: Know the enemy and know yourself; in a hundred battles you will never be in peril.

When you are ignorant of the enemy but know yourself, your chances of winning or losing are equal.

If ignorant both of your enemy and of yourself, you are certain in every battle to be in peril.

For to win one hundred victories in one hundred battles is not the highest skill. To subdue the enemy without fighting is the highest skill.

When birds of prey are attacking, they fly in low without extending their wings. When wild beasts are about to attack, they crouch low with their ears close to their heads. Similarly, when a sage is about to act, he always appears slightly dull.

Lin Hung-nien says a stone with no water within it is hard. A natural magnet with no water within it is dense. If a body is hard within and dense without, how can it ever be penetrated? If a thing has an opening, then it will be filled. If a thing has an inch of cavity, then one inch of water will fill it.

○ 古法大剛論章

再論吾所レ学此法度。理明二十時辰一。血脈安二分子午之法一。凡世人須下受二此法一止可上救レ人不レ可レ

害二人也一。有下人通二霊者一当中門之教上也。法有二軽重之殊一。故立下交二接之道一以レ熟能生中巧多上中。則彼

疎懶者必難レ用。凡有下与レ人打二枷一比中勢其理上一也。尤在二迅速一。不レ可レ作二児戯一。逢レ空則入。遇レ逃

則趄。須二斟酌一。恐レ失レ接。旁人視二之詔一我浅学二比勢者一顧二上下左右一分二作之門一。拳手之法。順則

用三草逆逆則用中確中遇上逃緊追。虎狼之勢。逢レ空緊入。逆二之則去一而来。順二之則来一去。在レ上用二蝴蝶双

飛一。在レ下用三撥水求レ魚妙手一。猛虎之威。交二手応一之法。在三着力認真暁得一。剛柔虚

実。剛来二柔中一。柔来二剛中一。剛刮柔発。身揺脚踏踢起身随二千門戸一。規矩進退不レ可二量情一是也。

○ 解脱法

欲レ攻東先打レ西。　　　　欲レ踏二前務随一後。　　欲レ転レ身剛二柔力一。　　髪被レ擒用二巨戟一。

欲レ攻レ他破二天柱一。　　他倒レ地頓二地勝一。　　我倒レ地入二他驕一。　　若レ抱二後天撞一後。

若レ抱二前遇一他陰一。　　扯二我臑一捐二他面一。　　殺二含泥一戟二他喉一。　　臨二吾身一用二吾樟一。

離二吾身一用二逆踏一。　　右欲レ捐二右先梢一　　脚欲レ踏二手先戟一。　　脚踢二高務随一後。

椀二吾手一用二吾梢一。　　槍二吾袖一用二戟樟一。　　牽二吾裾一用二膝脱一。　　欲レ踏レ我只用レ撲。

欲レ踢二他須一用レ釣一。　　他勢低勿レ用レ足。　　他勢高人二於中一。　　取二我下一乾二地上一

取二我上一随二地下一。　　扯二我髪一用二脱甲一。　　鎖二吾喉一用二大砍一。　　揺歩防レ来二他踢一。

手足相随方無レ失。

I was unable to locate the original source of the *kambun* [poetry in the Chinese style] that appears above. Several experts consulted felt that as it appears here, it may be incomplete or incorrect. For these reasons, I prefer not to impose my private interpretation on these passages and risk the transmission of inaccurate thoughts. Thus, I have not translated these Chinese sentences. [Translator's note.]